Spreading Light

"There are two ways of spreading light:
to be the candle or the mirror that reflects it."

Edith Wharton

Spreading Light

Religious Education for Special Children

Antonia Malone

Paulist Press ◇ *New York* ◇ *Mahwah*

For my children
Christopher, Mark, Monique,
Damian, Mike, Timmy,
Bonnie, Paul and Jenny

The Scripture quotations in this publication are from the *New American Bible*.

Library of Congress Cataloging-in-Publication Data

Malone, Antonia, 1935–
    Spreading light.

    Bibliography: p.
    1. Christian education of developmentally disabled
children.   I. Title.
BV1615.D48M35   1986   268'.0880826   86-2454
ISBN 0-8091-2798-9 (pbk.)

Published by Paulist Press
997 Macarthur Boulevard
Mahwah, New Jersey 07430

Printed and bound in the
United States of America

Contents

Contents

Part Three
Appendices

Acknowledgements

I wish to express my thanks to Freda Gardner, Associate Professor of Christian Education and the Director of the School of Christian Education at Princeton Theological Seminary, for her support and encouragement. Freda took the time to read the manuscript and suggest ways of presenting the material so that it would be suitable and/or adaptable for Protestant educators as well as those of my own Roman Catholic tradition. I hope I have successfully incorporated her suggestions.

Some years ago I took a continuing education course on methodology from Rev. Vincent Gartland, now of Toms River, New Jersey. It was this course which clarified my thinking on the principles of methodology for Christian education (hopefully, for all education). Application of his methods quickly proved the wisdom of his insights, many of which I have included in this book.

I also wish to thank my pastor, Monsignor Robert Bulman of St. Mary's Church, New Monmouth, New Jersey, who so generously supported and encouraged our center's efforts; Rev. Stanley Lukaszewski, our chaplain, whose cooperation and loving generosity made possible the many memorable liturgies we celebrated together; Joanne and Tom Gannon, my faithful co-workers for fifteen years; and my own nine children, most of whom were teachers and aides in our classrooms at one time or another.

And last, but not least, I must pay tribute to the members of the Monmouth County Holy Innocents Society and all the wonderful teachers, aides, parents and students who have been my friends and associates all these years and whose being present to me was the inspiration for much of this book.

O Lord, pour into us the Spirit of your love . . .

Henri Bissonnier

Introduction

The religious education of developmentally impaired children and youth is a ministry so specialized, because of the many different handicaps involved, that it is difficult (though not impossible) to plan a program and prepare a curriculum comprehensive enough to take into consideration the diverse situations with which one may have to deal. Over the last fifteen years our church's special religious education center has served blind children, deaf children, autistic children; children with Down's syndrome and hyperkinesis; children with multiple sclerosis, cerebral palsy and muscular dystrophy; perceptually impaired children and neurologically impaired children; children with multiple handicaps and hydrocephalic complications; children whose problems defy diagnosis and children whose diagnosis defies treatment. On request we have even included children with simple learning disabilities who, as they grow older and are unable to read at their age level, become increasingly more uncomfortable in a regular classroom situation.

These young people are as badly in need as anyone of the interaction, love, strength and solace provided by a warm and loving Christian community. Thus, it is not expedient to isolate them by teaching them individually or even in groups of two or three, and yet they need individual attention and affirmation. Because of the diversity of needs and the limited market, textbooks and teacher's manuals are few and cannot be comprehensively serialized, and yet these children need a structured and comprehensive program. This is the challenge facing the Christian religious education of special people today, as well as the challenge facing those who work with special children and youths and would like to pass on some of what they've learned through their years of experience in the field.

Sometimes the problems we have faced here at St. Mary's in New Monmouth have seemed insurmountable, but we have learned that the Holy Spirit has a particular interest in our special children, and somehow when surrendered in prayer our crosses always seem to turn into pluses.

It is this which has given me the courage to attempt to write this book, and it is my prayer that all who pick it up will find something in it for them. Over the years I have been researching available curriculum resources, attending workshops and visiting various centers of learning for special children. Lately, I have been giving workshops on much of the material in this book. Much of what I have learned has been incorporated into our program, altered and modified, the original sources perhaps forgotten. If someone reading this book recognizes herself or himself as one of the forgotten sources, I apologize for the lack of a footnote and would love to hear from you.

The chapters in this book have been explicitly titled so that you can find what you are looking for immediately. If you are just getting started with a new center, begin by reading Part I and reflect on it a while. Then read Part II, Chapter 4 and skim the rest of the book briefly. As you build your program, refer back to the chapters you need. It would be important for all your teachers to have copies of this book and for you to spend some time with them discussing the implications of Part I. When planning the opening workshop for your teachers, check with the How-To workshop I have included in the Appendix to make sure you have dealt with all aspects of the program.

If you have an established center, read Part I and then glance through the rest of the book, concentrating on those chapters which deal with problem areas in your program. Perhaps something you find will give you the inspiration to try something new. Over the years, we have experimented with almost anything for which someone else will vouch. The occasional resulting failures have been more than compensated for by the many unexpected successes. For instance, it took us a while before we realized that special children do marvelously with role playing and drama, and they love it. Learning by doing (especially if you're doing something you like to do) is learning at its best.

If you find that the curriculum materials available for the religious education of special children do not suit your needs, or if you have been through all the existing lesson plans you know of and need something new, be sure to read Chapters 6 and 7 and learn how to use available resources to write your own curriculum. Perhaps you can use some of the sample year plans as springboards for planning your own. Read Part I, analyze your needs and objectives, then glance through the samples and see what can be adapted for your center. Teachers of special children must be like good cooks who, though they have first learned to cook by following the recipe step by step, have now learned that with a little imagination they can adapt almost any recipe to suit their family's tastes.

If you are a Protestant, don't be put off by words such as "priest," "paraliturgy" and "First Holy Communion." There's nothing in this book which can't be adapted for your denominations. Again, like the good cook, survey your needs and the possibilities, then get together your team and let your imaginations give it a try. If your church is small, call the other churches in your area and invite their special children to join your group. The children will know each other from their schools, and it will work well.

I have avoided using the word retarded in this book as I am not sure the word carries a precise enough meaning anymore. As Will Rogers once quipped, "We're all retarded in our own way." Besides which the term "retard" has become a derogatory word in many young people's vocabulary, and I think it would be best to discontinue the use of it whenever possible.

Handicapped, though I will use it frequently, is only slightly better. While it is a more inclusive word, it depends for its definition on those who use it; thus there is always a danger of it being arbitrarily applied. After all, are we not all also handicapped in some way?

"Special education" as the term is used in our public school system refers to the education of all those who for one reason or another cannot fit into a regular classroom situation, and as these are the children who participate in our special religious education programs, I have, for want of a better word, decided to call them special children even though some are actually adolescents and young adults. Most special children will stay with a program such as ours until they leave school, or, if their handicaps are minor, until they can join a regular youth ministry program. However, there are always a few who remain with us into their twenties and maybe even thirties. These either stay with the young adult portion of our programs (ages about 16-20), or we promote them to the status of aides and find ways they can help around the classroom. Ideally, there should be a separate program for adults which special people could join when ready.

Part I of this book provides the basic material for reflection and action for all who would minister with special children, and Part II gives specific directions for starting a program, developing and training a teaching team and planning your programs and lessons.

The methodological principles specified in Part I are, for the most part, suitable for all persons as they are basic Christian education principles, but they are particularly important for our programs as they address the specific needs (often neglected in the past) of handicapped children and youth. Christian religious education cannot be separated from everyday life, for in its fullest sense Christian education is a way of helping people to live their whole lives in Christ Jesus. Thus we advocate a boldly demanding and solid program of religious formation aimed at promoting a totally Christian lifestyle.[1]

Special children respond wonderfully to such a challenge, partly, I think, because they intuit the truth and sense the work of the Spirit, and partly because such a program as described in these pages is a way of saying "we care," and "we love you."

People involved in a ministry with handicapped people quickly find that it is a ministry full of unexpected blessings. More often than not it is we teachers who are being ministered to by our students whose warm and affectionate natures are so endearing and whose struggles would be heartbreaking were it not for the light they spread so effectively.

"O Lord, pour into us the Spirit of your love."

Note

1. Henri Bissonnier, *The Pedagogy of Resurrection, The Religious Formation and Christian Education of the Handicapped and Maladjusted*, New York: Paulist Press, 1979, p. 4.

Prologue

Take a moment now and reflect . . . Today, whether we are working or playing, we live in a world of perpetual action, always rushing and short of time. In our educational efforts we also feel pressure. Common comments around religious education offices are, "There's too much to teach for just twenty lessons," "I haven't got time for this," "They don't even know the basics yet," "The year's almost over, and I haven't covered Pentecost," and "Sometimes I wonder if I've taught them anything."

To make the best use of available time and to keep our educational efforts fruitful, we must keep our priorities in order, and for this adequate reflection as well as careful planning is required. Tom Groome's "shared praxis"[1] method is admirably suited for this. No matter how long we have been teaching, regardless of what level, we must all pause on occasion and ask ourselves, preferably in dialogue with our associates: (1) What is the purpose of our Christian religious educating? (2) How is our religious educating being shaped by this purpose? (3) Is what we intended to happen by our educational methods actually happening?

Note

1. Thomas Groome, *Christian Religious Education*, San Francisco: Harper & Row, 1980.

Part One

Principles of Methodology

1

On the Purpose of Religious Education for Special Children

I think few people question anymore that all children have a right and a need for Christian religious education, and despite the fact that children with handicapping conditions are often particularly lovable, their parents know all too well that they're not all little saints. These are rather out-of-date considerations for anyone who is likely to pick up this book.

What parents of children with disabilities worry about most today and that which we must take into consideration is what's going to happen to their handicapped children when they grow up. How are they going to cope with a world which so often avoids and rejects them? Like all of us, handicapped people need to feel secure and loved, to have faith in their infinite value as human beings, to have hope in the future.

Special children are usually uninhibited when they are little, blithely unconscious of what people think of them. However, the older they get the more their differences set them apart from others their age, and then the problems multiply.

The foremost of these problems is that they become aware of being different. At this point two things can happen. Either they will learn to accept themselves as they are, and the chances are that they will keep their usually cheerful dispositions and be able to adjust to almost any circumstances, or they may refuse to accept themselves as they are, and either rebel outwardly or withdraw, either way setting themselves further apart from others.

Thus, the purpose of our religious educating must be to be a source of love and of hope to these children and their parents, to help to nurture in them a good self-image and enough internal strength so that they can cope with whatever life brings, and to assure them of their own potential to love and to adjust so that they will be able to accept themselves as they are, and know that what they are is good, lovable and capable.

Based on my years of experience in the field of special religious education, I am sure that if we can help to give our handicapped brothers and sisters the tools, the means, of listening to God, of knowing God's love within them, and of understanding his word, they will have self-respect, they will feel secure and loved, and they will be able to respond positively to a diversity of situations both now and in the years ahead. We have had special young adults in our classes who radiate such self-confidence and who take initiative socially to such an extent that after a few minutes in almost anyone's company their handicaps are no longer problematic. The road to such an achievement may be long and difficult, especially during the adolescent years, but it is the vision toward which we must be educating.

If this should seem a bit quixotic to some, it is worth noting that special children seem to have an affinity for the spiritual. When confronted with the good news, special children believe with that childlike simplicity and single-heartedness that Jesus recommends to all of us (Mt 18:1ff; 9:33; Lk 9:46ff). What seems mysterious and unreasonable to others, they often unquestionably accept.

This faith is a gift from God. It is the clay through which God is reaching out to us and with which we must work. It is a sacred responsibility.

"O Lord, pour into us the Spirit of your love."

2

On Shaping Our Educating
To Fit the Purpose

W hat can we do in our special religious education centers to help
our children grow in faith and confidence, to help our children
to be aware of and respond to God's initiative in their lives? What tools,
what means, will suit our purposes the best? Over the years I have come
to the conclusion that our efforts must be concentrated in three areas:
(1) affirmation; (2) community building; (3) getting to know Jesus.
Needless to say, these elements are interdependent.

Affirmation

If special children are to feel good about themselves, they need to
be constantly affirmed, and if this affirmation is to be specifically
Christian, it will be an affirmation of both their lovableness and their
God given potential.

Simple affirmation strategies grounded in the teachers' own faith
from which teachers reach out to share their faith and love with their
students will help students to feel both lovable and capable. Affirmation
can be expressed both through method and content.

A list of methodological affirmation strategies might read as follows. Perhaps you can add a few of your own.

1. *No Wrong Answers*. The successful presentation of any theme
depends on constant interaction between teacher and students. People
learn best, says educator Donald Rogers, when they are listened to and
when they think that what they are saying is a worthwhile contribution
to the discussion.[1]

Children who are told that their answers or comments are wrong
will very likely never raise their hands again, nor will their friend in the
next seat who is observing the put-down. To create a non-threatening
atmosphere for dialogue as well as a lively exchange, it is perfectly pos-

sible to field any answer in a positive way. Such encouraging remarks as "You're on the right track," "What a good idea! I hadn't thought of that," or "I see what you mean. Now what would you say if . . . " (and give them a clue to the answer you are looking for) make it possible for you to lead the children to the desired answer and still let them know that they have made a contribution to the class discussion.

If the answer given is difficult to turn around or redirect, rather than drawing attention to the child's error, you might focus for a minute on what the child was thinking, thus affirming his thoughts. For example: You've told the story of the exodus and the ten commandments. The next week in the follow-up you ask: Who remembers the story of the ten commandments? Some hands go up, and they tell you a little of what they remember. (This would have been a good lesson for the students to dramatize.) You ask if anyone remembers the name of the man to whom God gave the tablet with the ten commandments on it? Who was the leader of the people? A student answers, "Father Smith," which is the name of your parish priest. Now you might say, "Oh, yes, Father Smith is a leader, and he could tell us all about the ten commandments," and you continue talking for a few minutes about Father Smith, comparing his relationship to the community with that of Moses' and his people. Then you can begin again, "And who was this man who first gave God's commandments to his people? I'll give you a clue. His name begins with MO . . . "

As important as a positive approach to verbal responses is an appreciation of non-verbal and/or symbolic responses. This is not at all unusual with special children who often find it difficult to express themselves verbally or who do not talk. At the end of a recent year, our group was sitting in a circle and discussing what we had accomplished this year and what we liked most about our special education community. After a few hesitant answers from students, a teenager tried with difficulty to say something. Suddenly realizing that she was having difficulty expressing herself, she got up, came over to me and embraced me. At this everyone suddenly seemed very happy, for we all understood what Lisa had expressed in gesture was just what we all wanted to say.

2. *Sunshine Calls*. After the first few weeks of religion classes, call your students' parents or group parents. On hearing who is on the phone, parents will immediately worry. Something must be wrong if the teacher is calling. But contrary to their expectations, you say,

"Good morning, Mrs. Jones. I'm Jane Smith, Jim's religion teacher. I just thought I'd call you up to say hello and see if you have any questions about our program . . . and I wanted to tell you how pleased we are to have Jim in our class." And then you tell her something you like about Jim and perhaps something clever or helpful he said or did in class.

The usual result of this strategy is that the mother feels great and tells everyone about the phone call at the dinner table. As a result the father beams at Jim, Jim is proud of himself, and all his brothers and sisters are wishing that their religion teachers would call and say something nice about them—as well they should. The following week Jim comes eagerly to religion class, anxious to learn and participate, confident that his teacher cares about him and that he can handle it.

This should of course never be regarded as a gimmick. Even the most annoying child has redeeming characteristics if you look for them, and an exercise such as this one is a good reminder to us to take note of these features.

3. *Say-So.* A say-so has similar results to a sunshine call. A say-so is a simple affirmation directly to the child such as a hug, an "I love you," or "I think that drawing you made is great. Let's hang it up." It might include such little things as putting stars or smiling faces on papers or drawings. It seems so obvious, and yet so many of us have unwittingly been so well trained to criticize, correct and improve that it takes some intentional reflection and reacting before affirmation becomes a natural role.

4. *Displaying Work.* Displaying the children's work in the classroom, at a liturgy or prayer service (paraliturgy), or at a social event to which parents, siblings and friends have been invited will help to give the children a sense of accomplishment, and can be accompanied by singing a song for the parents or perhaps even a dramatization of a parable or other Bible story.

5. *Identifying Strengths.* As we are not teachers of academics, it is not necessary that we constantly work on improving our students' weak points. Concentrate instead on their talents and strong points and the chances are that the weak ones will improve also. If some children are good at drawing, praise their drawings and ask them if they'd like to illustrate the lesson on the board with some simple drawings. Children who can read, play an instrument or sing should have the opportunity to do so at liturgies. Make it a point to find out what each child

can do. Everyone can do something—light a candle, carry the Bible, find the reading, sharpen pencils, pass out papers, tell a story, say a prayer, help move chairs or fix refreshments. Let the children help each other whenever possible even if it takes longer. Everyone needs to feel both useful and capable, so be careful that you don't do too much for them. Better a sloppy paper or a simpler arts and crafts project than one the teacher did for them.

Affirmation is also implicit in the lesson content. The understanding of our Christian faith held by the teacher will undoubtedly be that which is passed on to the students. While we do not expect to teach explicit theology in the classroom, our own understanding of the meaning of being created in the image of God, of sin, of grace, of fundamental option, of prayer, of salvation, of justice and mercy, will be implicit in everything we do and say—in particular, in the way we present our lessons. Thus, it is important that we know what we believe and that we have a positive up-to-date theological outlook.

We have lived too long with the God who is shaking his finger at us from somewhere above the clouds while he admonishes us as to all the things we shouldn't do. Hopefully we have heard the last of such threats as "God will punish you," and "If you do that again, you'll surely go to hell." If we can concentrate instead on being redeemed people, forgiving and forgiven people, people of hope, people created in the image of God, people through whom God seeks to transform the world, we will be giving our students strength for the future and affirming their infinite human value.

Rather than compiling lists of do's and don'ts, simple drawings with stick figures can illustrate that we live within the encompassing love of a God who creates us to journey toward him, and that when we deliberately step outside the rays of his love or reject the voice of God within ourselves, discord arises both in our lives and in our hearts. And so we sin, and the results are not good.

This lesson can be illustrated in dialogue from incidents or hypothetical happenings in our students' lives and accompanied by a related Scripture storytelling or reading of the prodigal son (Lk 15), the lost sheep (Lk 15) or Jesus' command to Peter, "Follow me" (Jn 21:19). A prayer service in which we express our sorrow for the times we have walked away from God and celebrate the joy of reconciliation would be a good conclusion to such a lesson.

This lesson could be followed up with a lesson on forgiveness and reconciliation and/or a communal penance service.

A lesson on creation is an affirming way to begin the year. After a dramatic reading of excerpts from Genesis 1, which you have illustrated with pictures and interpolated with teacher-student dialogue, point out how much God must love us if he made us in his image: how to God each person is precious, unique and irreplaceable. Follow this with a discussion of the gifts God has given each of us. Go around the class pointing out some of the students' gifts. For example, "God gave Maria pretty blonde hair," "God gave John a beautiful smile." Let the students contribute their ideas on the subject.

The following week, as the children are working in the small groups, take their pictures individually. Hopefully you can locate a Polaroid-type camera for this. Each group can then decorate a piece of poster board with their pictures, their names, and symbols of what their group is concentrating on that year. These pictures could be arranged around a picture of Jesus, a picture of bread and wine, a confirmation symbol, etc. Under each picture have students, aides or teachers list some of the gifts each child has. Some children, in particular the older ones, may want to add some accomplishments to this list, such as "God helped make Pat a great bowler." These posters, if displayed all year at liturgies and community get-togethers, are great conversation pieces and a source of affirmation for the students. This lesson could be completed by forming a prayer group and thanking God for his gifts.

A preceding or follow-up lesson on creation could discuss the responsibility God has given us by entrusting the stewardship of the earth to us. If possible take a walk with the students and note the beauty of the world. If this is not possible, use pictures or bring in objects such as a flower, a leaf, etc. This might lead to a discussion of pollution and our personal responsibility to care for the earth. Thus we try not to be litterbugs, throw bottles and paper out of car windows, etc. An art project stressing ways of caring for the earth would be appropriate.

Confirmation students participating in such a lesson might decide as part of their community service project to help clean up the church yard or some other community area.

These are just a few illustrations of how lesson contents can affirm your students. The method is not to avoid the negative issues (such as sin, pollution, or injustice) as if they didn't exist, but to place them in contexts which stress positive options (such as forgiveness, reconciliation, service to others).

And God looked at everything he had made and he found it very good (Genesis 1:31).

Community Building

"If our children are to have faith," says Christian educator John Westerhoff, "we need to make sure that the church becomes a significant community of faith." Westerhoff goes on to say that our church communities must be small enough to be intimate and composed of at least three generations.[2]

While the sizes of many of our parishes and churches preclude such intimacy developing at a parish level, smaller communities within the church or parish, such as our special education centers, can function as the "significant community of faith" that Westerhoff describes. In fact, they must do so, for special children perhaps more than anyone need the security of an intimate Christian community as they are so often on the fringes of other communal-type activities. Parents, grandparents, siblings, teachers, aides and students can all have a role in such a community if the opportunity is afforded them through the structuring of our programs to include not only teaching moments, but also worship moments, social moments and opportunities for service.

1. *The teaching moment*, the one with which we are most familiar, is adequately covered throughout this book and may well be the central moment around which the center's activities revolve. The only precaution we might take in this regard is to remember not to let our classrooms turn into parodies of the children's academic classrooms. Though some might debate this, religion is not just another subject with a list of required facts to memorize and a set curriculum that, no matter what, must be completed on schedule. Hopefully, in our centers through the practice of affirmation, community building and sharing of our Christian story and vision,[3] whatever our children need to nurture their growth in faith will be absorbed and become part of their lives. And, with the help of the Spirit, it is our experience that this is the case. In fact, it is our experience that the faith of the children has brought a

growth in faith to all who are part of our community. Teachers, aides, parents and grandparents have found their faith renewed and nourished through their participation in our center's activities, particularly in our worshipping moments.

2. "*Worship* symbolizes the process of God's presence and our response," says educator priest Regis Duffy.[4] It is an ongoing call to Christian conversion and commitment and thus central to the educating process as it calls us to examine what it means *for us* to be a Christian in the world today. We are reminded of Matthew's example, "If you bring your gift to the altar and there recall that your brother has anything against you, leave your gift at the altar and go first to be reconciled with your brother, and then come and offer your gift" (Mt 5:23–24). "It is no accident," says Fr. Duffy, "that this moment of personal awareness occurs at worship."[5]

If we then hope to bring our children to an awareness of God's presence with the hope that they will respond and grow in Christian commitment, we must make available to them moments for worship.

Liturgies and prayer services prepared especially for and by our children to which parents, grandparents, friends and siblings are invited are the best of teaching moments. If these are concluded with refreshments, they become social moments, and if they are the occasion of a food collection for the needy or a reception for senior citizens, they also become service moments. Their effectiveness will depend on our commitment to the centrality of worship in our lives and our willingness to let the liturgies be the students' expression. Let the children enjoy worship. Don't suppress their exuberance. "Enter into it and wonderful things will happen."[6]

Sociologists remind us that the rituals of worship arise originally as the expression of people's religious feelings. As these rituals become routine, and the next generation comes along, they are simply imposed on the next generation rather than being the expression of the next generation's religious feelings. This could explain why you so often hear the complaint that our church rituals are not "meaningful" to young people. Now I grant you that this kind of remark can be an excuse not to make the faith search to which we are all called, but nevertheless the point has value, as we should be aware that different kinds of people need to express their religious feelings in different manners. Of no one is this more true than of special children.

There is plenty of room within our liturgical frameworks for original, personal and communal expression. Students can help pick an appropriate theme (perhaps something they're studying), do the readings, make and bring up gifts, serve at the altar, prepare the prayers, make the decorations (banners, posters, garlands, etc.), pass out programs, choose the music, play simple rhythm instruments, form a procession, dramatize the Gospel, and interact with the homilist. A meditation can be distributed to the parents for quiet moments which should also be a part of every worship experience. A reflective type hymn can prepare students for the quiet moments.

Before Easter you might have a service focusing on the Last Supper and for refreshments serve several different kinds of bread. During Lent you might have a communal penance service focusing on the meaning of reconciliation and as a sign forego the refreshments.

The ideal time for these worship moments is during or after class time, although for special events such as First Holy Communion or confirmation you may want to set aside a special date. Time and frequency will depend on the availability of a priest or minister and a chapel, church or room for celebrating. However, once a month is not too often. Paraliturgies (prayer services) are also effective and can be used instead.

If your group is too small for its own celebration, consider joining with a pre-school or first grade class if your children are little, or with an older group if they are more adult. As the children begin to feel comfortable and confident at these celebrations, you can consider placing a notice in the church bulletin noting the time and place of your liturgy and welcoming all in the larger community who would like to participate.

You will find that these liturgies are a good preparation for the children's participation in the larger churches' community worship experiences. Suggest to parents that they take their children regularly to the same service on Sundays so that they get to know people and to feel as if they belong.

3. *Social moments,* in addition to the monthly liturgies, might include annual Communion lunches or breakfasts; family and/or community outings to the circus, ice shows, local fairs and events; a yearly picnic or swimming party; a weekly bowling or basketball program. In many areas of the country there are a limited number of organized activities for special children, in particular inexpensive or free programs. Parents of special children often find their resources drained by medical

bills. Thus a weekly sports program sponsored by a church or charitable group would probably be most welcome. Don't be afraid to approach possible sponsoring organizations. If they can't do it, they'll probably find you someone who will. Parents might be willing to help organize a bowling program, and teenagers are the best of aides if allowed to bowl with the children.

4. *Community service moments* are not beyond special children, but must simply be geared to their abilities. It would be a mistake to always allow our children to be the recipients of other organizations' good will and never to take the initiative in service. Instead of having the youth group give a picnic for special children every year, let your center give a party or put on a skit for the youth group or, even better, for the senior citizens in your parish and/or community. Let everyone have at least a small part in the preparations. Even if dividing up the chores in this way is time-consuming, it's a worthwhile endeavor when you see how pleased the children are with their accomplishments.

Simple gifts prepared for nursing home patients at Christmas time, cards for Easter or Valentine's day, and food collections for the church pantry are all easy ways for our children to realize that they are capable of giving and serving as well as receiving.

Community building games at the beginning of the year facilitate the development of community. Why not open the year with a picnic or worship service or both? An outdoor liturgy can be beautiful. Then while the children are playing some simple getting-to-know-you games, have an adult ice-breaker for the parents. Parents of special children have much in common and are anxious to share their concerns with other parents. After the ice-breaker they quickly become at ease with each other, and you will find community building happening at every event with a minimum of effort on your part.[7]

And don't forget to use the talents of everyone involved. The biggest mistake that leaders of such groups could make would be to think they have to do it all themselves. Discover the talents of co-workers, parents, and aides, and don't be afraid to ask them to take on responsibilities. Every group needs a grandmother with an available lap for hugging and loving the child who can't cope with the class that day. Every center needs a man with whom the adolescent boys can relate.

Nor should the group be so structured that there is no opportunity for a student to seek out a teacher for a heart-to-heart talk. Adolescents often need an adult outside of the family circle in whom they can confide. A relaxed atmosphere and enough teachers and aides so that there is always someone available just to talk will make adolescents feel comfortable in your group.

And don't forget your teenage helpers. They are wonderful one-on-one with that physically handicapped or hyperactive child who needs a little extra assistance.

> *There are different gifts, but the same Spirit. There are different ministries, but the same Lord; there are different works, but the same God who accomplishes all of them in everyone. To each person the manifestation of the Spirit is given for the common good. . . . You then are the body of Christ. Everyone of you is a member of it (1 Cor 12:4–7, 27).*

Getting To Know Jesus

A Christian community is only effective in transforming and empowering its members if there is an awareness of the Spirit of Jesus dwelling in its midst. The forms that this awareness takes is what we call spirituality. All members of a community are called to a personal relationship with God and Jesus, and the common denominator in these relationships is that they lead us to love one another. Thus, the essential complement to community is our spirituality, our relationship with God and his Son Jesus.

But how, we ask, do we help our young people to develop such a relationship? Indeed, how do we ourselves develop such a relationship? As I shall later illustrate, to develop a relationship with someone implies getting to know them. In this section I would like to discuss three primary ways we get to know Jesus—through Scripture, prayer and sacrament—and I would like to indicate how best to utilize these elements in our special religious education centers.

It is through Jesus that we know God as Father. As far as scholars know, people never used the word Father to describe their image of God before Jesus. In this way Jesus radically changed humanity's perception of God.

It is also through Jesus that we come to know ourselves. In our solidarity with the humanity of Jesus we begin to perceive our own true nature, our own potentiality, and what it means to be Christian. Children, as well as all of us, can identify with the Jesus who enjoyed the company of his friends and an occasional party (Jn 2:1–12), but who could also cry at the death of his friend Lazarus, get tired of crowds, get angry with the Pharisees for making life difficult for the poor, and be willing to help the sick, the sinner and the outcasts of society, and who suffered and died himself an outcast.

As we introduce our students to the Jesus who had a bias for the poor, the wounded, the suffering, those living on the fringes of society, we must pass on the good news that Jesus is still with us today. Jesus can heal today as he did on this earth many years ago, if we place our trust in him and recognize him in our midst.

This is not to suggest to blind children that Jesus will restore their sight nor to lame children that they will walk. Such promises, while not out of the realm of possibility, are not ours to make, as only God knows how he chooses to heal. But we can promise our children that if they place their faith and life in God's hands, they will find peace and reconciliation with the world despite their handicaps.

We might remind them that physical healing isn't the answer to all our problems. Other things bother us too. After Jesus cured the blind man, that man's problems quickly multiplied. Now not only was he in trouble with the Pharisees and the temple priest, but he was suddenly responsible for making a whole new life for himself which would have its own problems. No longer could he sit begging by the gate. Instead he would have to join the crowd looking for employment.

This may seem like risky ground for a teacher to tread on, but we can't go on forever deleting the passages on healing from the Bible. One way or another we're going to have to come to terms with our own understanding of healing so that when one of our students asks us why Jesus hasn't healed him or her, we won't be struck dumb.

It is our task then to bring our students to the healing love of Jesus, to the source of our reconciliation both with God and with ourselves, our problems and our world. To reveal his healing presence in our midst was the task of the Gospel writers, and it is to them that we must turn for inspiration.

Scripture

No lesson is complete unless it is rooted in Scripture, surrendered to prayer and celebrated as a sign of God's presence among us. No classroom is complete without a Scripture corner in which the Bible is reverentially displayed. The latter can be portable and set up in a minute or two. (Let the children take turns doing this.) All you need is a cloth, table, candle, Bible and Bible stand. The area could on occasion be decorated with flowers or the students' art work.

Scripture reading or storytelling should be preceded by a discussion of what book this is, what it contains, how we got it, etc. Analogies of our present storytelling procedures to those which preceded the composition of the Gospel enhance the reality of our stories in the children's eyes. As special children benefit from repetition and are happy when they can make known their knowledge, do this every week. You can add little bits of practical interest which relate to that particular day's readings. For this a good dictionary of the Bible or a one volume commentary is a worthwhile investment.[8] You need not pass on all your research to the children, but it will help clarify your own understanding as you plan the presentation. (For how to prepare a presentation see Chapter 7.)

If your day's theme revolves around a Bible story, be prepared to illustrate it with a variety of materials. Illustrate a dramatic reading or storytelling with pictures, flannel board figures, puppets, chalkboard illustrations, song, music and/or audio-visual materials such as slides. Filmstrips and movies can be used without the sound. With this the teacher supplies the script, choosing words that are understandable and speaking at a moderate pace.

Good storytellers must have a bit of the actor/actress in them. Carrying the Bible, add motions and intonations appropriate to the reading. Bring the story to life in your presentation. Interject questions and comments relating the content to your students' lives. Invite the children to retell the story using pictures and/or flannel board or to act it out while you reread it.

If your Scripture reading is used to reinforce your presentation, such as in the lesson previously discussed on sin and our relationship to God, light the candle, then ask everyone to sit quietly and listen to the word of the Lord on what has been discussed. As you read, carefully point out the connection and elicit comments. Often the connection is self-evident and you can let the students point it out to you. This can then flow into spontaneous prayer or a guided prayer meditation. This works particularly well with children ages ten and up. With little ones a dramatic storytelling may be more effective. This can, of course, also flow into prayer.

The question often arises as to how much it is permissible to simplify, abridge or change the wording of Scripture in the reading or telling of it. If you are doing a storytelling without using the Bible you can, of course, be more creative. However, you may want afterward to point out where the story is in the Bible and perhaps even read it aloud. This will facilitate the children's ability to recognize the reading when they hear it in church.

If you are telling the story by reading directly from the Bible, I find no objection to abridging (all of Genesis 1 would certainly be too long for our children) or to substituting easier words for more difficult ones. I would hesitate only to change the story to the extent that it no longer bears enough resemblance to the original to be recognizable at Sunday worship or to the extent that you might even unintentionally distort the meaning. (The children love it when at Sunday worship they recognize one of the readings.)

Help the children to appreciate the beauty of the wording of many of our best translations of the Bible by pointing out the meaning of words. Don't underestimate the ability of the beauty and poetry of the original to reach the children regardless of their handicap. There are many graces involved with Scripture reading which make possible the seemingly impossible, and as you proceed you will become aware of this. "Let the little children come to me" (Mk 10:14).

Prayer

Doris Donnelly, Catholic theologian, author and educator, reminds us that prayer is a relationship, and like every relationship it develops as the parties involved get to know each other. Prayer like other relationships has its seasons, its good times and its bad.[9] Our prayer life deepens as we meet Jesus and God in Scripture, then recognize them in ourselves and others, and finally hear them speak to us in our hearts as we speak to them. Our task is to guide the children to the awareness of their presence and the realization that to those who seek, they are always available. Similarly, we must point out that God communicates with us through nature as does his Son through other people (Mt 25:35–45).

There are many ways of responding to God's initiative, and we should introduce the children to a variety of ways of praying, remembering always that we may never be sure in which way God will touch them.

The value of memorized prayers such as the Our Father lies not only in their beauty and their comprehensiveness, but in their availability for community prayer and for moments when we don't know what to say or pray. Memorized formal prayers are good for beginning pray-ers and for meditation. As these are the prayers the children are most likely to use at home, we should encourage their use in the classroom.

Spontaneous prayer can flow from any lesson or Scripture reading. Light a candle, take a moment for all to make themselves comfortable, then reflect together on the day's lesson. A lesson on creation may flow into a prayer of thanks for God's gifts. Don't be concerned if the children are thanking God mostly for their pets. It's a natural after reading Genesis 1, and who's to say how much a pet may mean to a special child. Pets can be very affectionate, and special children crave affection.

A lesson on the commandment to love one another might flow into prayers of petition to help us to love and to forgive. A lesson on Jesus' healing and miracles might lead to prayers of intercession for the sick, especially for those in our families. If you have trouble quieting the children down for prayer time, put on some reflective music and ask them to relax and listen for a few minutes.

In preparation for a communal penance service, one might have a prayer service illustrating the effect of God's forgiveness using rituals such as "burning our sins." After discussing our relationship with God and Jesus and what turning away from God does to us, light a candle, then read an appropriate Scripture passage and have the children take a moment to reflect on their lives and whether they have been following the way of love. Younger children can be asked to run (in their imaginations) a movie of their day's activities. As you guide them through their day, ask them how they reacted to the various challenges of home, school and play. For older children a more appropriate, more grown-up examination of conscience can be prepared.

Now have the children indicate on a piece of paper by symbol, drawing or writing (aides can help if necessary) something they did wrong and are sorry about. Emphasize that no one is going to see what is on the paper except them, so it doesn't matter how their efforts look. These papers are then folded and placed in an empty coffee can near the Bible and candle and a moment of silent prayer asking God's forgiveness follows. Perhaps an appropriate song for reflection could be played. The papers are then ignited, and the children silently watch the conflagration as the music plays. Little need be said of the symbolism involved unless you are asked. Most special children seem to understand intuitively.

Guided prayer meditations are effective with all ages. There are some available books of guided prayer meditations, none of which are designed for special children, but any of which will give you ideas on how to prepare your own. A few are listed at the end of this chapter.[10]

The theme of the meditation should reflect the relationship we have experienced with Jesus in the day's Scripture and presentation. After the Scripture passage has been read, ask all present to relax, close their eyes, take a few deep breaths, fold their hands and imagine themselves in a special place or situation. (The place depends on the setting of the meditation and the theme you are developing, but it should be a place they like to be and has meaning for them.) The leader asks the students to allow Jesus to become present to them in a special way, to visualize him in their mind's eye coming to join them in this special place. The leader might ask them to imagine Jesus speaking to them, to talk to him and to listen for his response. A period of silence follows. This can be concluded with appropriate reflective music. The children should be reminded afterward that they can return to this special place and speak with Jesus whenever they pray.

Guided prayer meditations work best with small groups (under twenty) and with adolescents and young adults. Nevertheless, we do them every year with small children also, as it introduces them to the idea of a two-way communication, a personal relationship with Jesus. As it is difficult with small children to maintain the total silence one would like for such meditations, it is better to separate older and younger children for such an activity. If you have a particularly active or disruptive child in the classroom you may want to have an aide take him or her for a walk during this prayer moment, but don't do this indiscriminately because it is our experience that often the noisiest child, the one you least expect to participate, enjoys such a meditation and is unbelievably quiet for the duration. I think I would always give it a try first. If it doesn't work out, you can always try again another day. Reflective music helps. There are many handicapped children who will immediately settle down, just like you or me, if a quiet inspirational song is played.

Jesus at Gethsemane showed us that prayer is a source of strength through which our inner turmoils can be resolved. He tells us continually that if we ask, we shall receive (Mt 7:7–11). We would be sadly remiss if we failed to share our belief in the power of prayer with our students.

If you live in me, and my words stay part of you, you may ask what you will, and it will be done for you (Jn 15:7).

Sacrament

Sacramental moments, since they are worship moments, symbolize the presence of God, of grace welling up in our communities, uniting us in Christ Jesus, and they memorialize shared moments in ours and Jesus' life. Sacramental moments should thus be celebrated as part of community worship.

The best lesson one could give on baptism is to plan for the baptism of a sibling or member of the community during a community liturgy. In addition, or as an alternative, one could role-play a baptism in class. Repeat the ceremony several times so that each child has a turn to take part. Students will take the roles of parents, godparents, priest, and congregation. You will need a doll, basin, water, candle and white baptismal robe or cover of some sort. Keep it short, stressing the baptismal promises and the actual baptism.

A communal penance service should be part of each year's plan. When penance is properly presented as an opportunity for reconciliation with God, we find the children willing and anxious to go to confession. Needless to say, no one is compelled to go, and the confession is always face to face. In fact, with little ones it is often on the priest's lap. While most little children and some of the older ones are not of an age to grasp the full significance of the sacrament, it is our experience that everyone wants to participate, at the very least to have those few private moments with Father Smith.

As all our celebrations are for the whole community, it is conducive to a reverential attitude to have music playing during confessions and perhaps to hand out a meditation for the parents. It is at celebrations such as these that we have observed parents and other community members, after many years' absence, return to the sacraments.

Communion and confirmation celebrations should also be part of community liturgies. Depending on your situation you may want to celebrate these moments with the larger church community. I would, however, beware of having children suddenly included in a huge celebration if they know no one, are ill at ease and cannot take an active part. As these are joyful, prayer-filled moments, they should be celebrated in whichever way the children will experience them as joyful and prayerful.

You will find some suggestions for penace and Communion celebrations in Appendix II. There are also some good books on children's liturgies from which you may adapt ideas for your own celebrations. Some of these are listed in the annotated bibliography.

In Chapters 6 and 7 on planning, you will note that sacramental celebrations, if we hope to present them as ways of meeting Jesus, must be preceded by appropriate lessons which indicate their origin and their function in our lives. In preparation for Communion the week before Easter would be a good time to have a role-play of the Last Supper. Have the children sit on the floor or around a long table. Let them take turns being Jesus. As you read the Scripture account first from John for the footwashing, then from Matthew, Mark or Luke for the blessing of the bread and wine, let them act it out and say the key words (such as "This is my body"). A basin and towel, pita bread, grape juice, clay chalice and plate (or perhaps a more elaborate one borrowed from the church), and a cloak for Jesus are all you need. Afterwards point out the analogy to the liturgy of the Eucharist. Then, if you have time, someone could be Father Smith and act out his role also.

Where two or three are gathered in my name, there am I in the midst of them (Mt 18:20).

Summary

Affirmation, community building and getting to know Jesus are then the key points around which our planning and methodology must revolve if we hope to help our children grow in faith and confidence. If we fail to affirm our children, we will not be able to build community, for they will withdraw and the joy and spontaneity which are part of

Christian community will not be realized. If we fail to build community, our educating efforts will become just another compartment of our students' lives, something they do once a week or one period a day, called "religion," but which bears no relation to the totality of their lives. If we fail to help our students to develop a personal relationship with Jesus, the connection between Jesus and their lives will be lost to them. They will not really know him, and their faith will not be receiving the nourishment that it is our task to provide.

Notes

1. Donald Rogers, *In Praise of Learning,* Nashville, Abingdon Press, 1980.

2. John Westerhoff, *Will Our Children Have Faith?* N.Y., Seabury Press, 1976, p. 54.

3. Thomas Groome, *Christian Religious Education,* San Francisco, Harper and Row, 1980.

4. Regis Duffy, *Real Presence,* N.Y., Harper and Row, 1982, p. 40.

5. *Ibid.,* p. 41.

6. Dorothy Clark, Jane Dahl, Lois Gonzenback, *Teach Me, Please Teach Me,* Elgin, Ill., David Cook Publishing Co., 1974, p. 14.

7. Two good books on group building for any ages are: Andrew Fluegelman (ed.), *The New Games Book,* N.Y., Doubleday, 1976; Lyman Coleman, *Handbook of Serendipity,* Colorado Springs, Serendipity House, 1976.

8. John L. McKenzie, *Dictionary of the Bible,* Milwaukee, The Bruce Publishing Co., 1965. *Jerome Biblical Commentary* and other commentaries are available at your Church's religious bookstore.

9. Doris Donnelly, from a lecture, New Monmouth, N.J., December 1982.

10. Anthony Mello, *Sadhana,* available also on tape. Order both from The Institute of Jesuit Sources, 3700 West Pine, St. Louis, Missouri, 63108, $5 paperback; Maxie Dunnam, *The Workshop of Living Prayer,* Nashville, The Upper Room, 1974. For additional resources see: *The Friendly Classroom for a Small Planet,* Priscilla Prutzman, *et al.*

3

Evaluating Your Efforts

The biggest danger in our religious education programs is that we as teachers get so wrapped up in what we are doing and so convinced of the rightness of it all that we fail to take the time to check whether our efforts are actually bearing fruit. In a way I hate to say this, as I do not doubt that Jesus will bless our best intentions as he so often does, but, being human, we must always beware of the seed of self-righteousness, which is so difficult to exorcise from our hearts.

A professional special education teacher of whom I once read tells of the time and patience involved in teaching her special children to read. Laboriously, after many weeks they learn the letters C, A, T. After a while they learn that in this combination they spell "cat." And then one day when least expected they connect "cat" with that little animal running around at home, and *that* is when learning takes place.

And so it is with religion. We can teach our students any number of things which they may even be able to repeat, but until they become part of our children's lives, till they connect with what is going on at home, at school and on the playground and have become part of the totality of their life experience, they are meaningless to them.

But how do we evaluate whether this has taken place? Jesus tells us that by their fruits you shall know them, and I think that as we watch our children grow in faith and confidence in our communities, it will become obvious that good things are happening. But what about more immediate checks? Checks along the way?

An effective way of checking on learning might be in follow-up sessions after a lesson or story on Jesus' life. Pose some real-life situations which necessitate a choice of action, and ask the children which course of action they would choose. With the older or less handicapped students you might ask why they chose this course of action. If the responses indicate a lack of understanding of the lesson they were intended to illustrate, you will have to reconsider your presentation. Does it just need reinforcing? Did you fail to point out the relation of the story to their life experience? Did you misread their life experience? Or was the subject matter, perhaps, beyond the comprehension level of the students?

As you check make notations on all your lesson plans and keep them from year to year. If a certain presentation fails to elicit the desired response, even when reinforced, you might question the wisdom of using it again. Remember that different groups of students may respond differently to the same presentation.

It is extremely important to know as much as possible about your students' lives if you hope to make the desired connections. If you talk about the church as a good mother, and the child's mother has deserted the family, you have used an unfortunate analogy. If you talk about Jesus as shepherd and your children have never seen sheep, much less a shepherd, you might have trouble making clear the importance of the shepherd to his flock of sheep.

The comprehension level of your students is also difficult to gauge although employing the above checks will eventually give you a feel for it. Some understanding of human developmental studies will also help. For instance, most special children, though not all, never reach what Jean Piaget in his studies of cognitive development calls the stage of formal operations.[1] This stage which the average child reaches about the age of ten to fourteen is characterized by the ability to reason about abstract concepts: an abstract concept being an idea or reality which you cannot image or concretely perceive. For this reason an understanding of an abstract concept, such as the Trinity, is beyond young children and beyond most of our special children no matter how clever the analogy you employ. Unlike "cat" you can't attach "Trinity" to an acceptable concrete God image. You will notice that in acknowledgement of this cognitive problem most manuals for young children under the age of ten now speak of Jesus as "our brother" rather than God.

Similarly, they do not tell children that God is spirit, for to tell children that God is spirit is also to introduce an abstract concept. Most children image God as an elderly gentleman looking something like a grandfather. This should not be surprising if we consider that in their eyes if God is the grown Jesus' father, he must be an old man. Add to this the fact that he has always existed, and we have, indeed, a very old man.

More problematic is imaging the Holy Spirit. Are they to think of the Holy Spirit as the invisible man? a bird or dove? a ghost? As we must deal with the concept of the Spirit, I have found it best to speak of the Holy Spirit as the Spirit of Jesus. This I find is theologically adequate at their level and helps the children image the Spirit (if they must) without distortion.

"Being happy" and "love" are also abstract concepts, but special children have no trouble grasping these if they have been concretized for them in act or symbol. Thus "love" means the good feeling when mother hugs them, and a drawing of a heart symbolizes this good feeling. Similarly, "being happy" means having a party, and a picture of children having fun symbolizes "being happy."

Symbols, then, help concretize abstract concepts to the extent that they can be related to a child's real life experience, and they are good teaching tools to this extent only. A dove for the Spirit, then, remains a problem, but other religious symbols such as a candle for light, water for washing, and bread and wine for food and drink are less problematic. If you are alert to these cognitive difficulties, you will begin to notice which symbols you can effectively employ in your lesson plans. Outside of these, it is best to ask the students to employ their reasoning only with matters that can be related to a concrete image or reality.

On the other hand, while we must judiciously deal with abstract concepts, we must also be aware that reason is not the only way to God. All children are capable of intuitive knowledge from their earliest years although they may not always be able to express or reason about what they know. For this reason it is important in spiritual matters not to continually press children to explain themselves and to leave room in our expectations for the work of the Spirit. A recent study in England indicated that thousands of adults have, as children, had religious experiences which have had a lifelong effect on them. Such an experience is not an abstract concept for the one involved but a reality—although a mysterious one. Therefore, whatever you do, do not be afraid to challenge your students. With the help of the Spirit they are infinitely more capable than they are usually credited to be. The problem is that this is not always obvious, and thus we get discouraged easily and underestimate their capabilities as well as our own.

We have had mothers of children who never speak in class, although they may speak at home, say to us as Ellen's mother did, "My husband and I can't understand why, but Ellen learns more in her one hour of religion a week than she does five days a week at school."

Why does Ellen talk at home but never with us? Why does she

seem to absorb more in religion class than in her academic classes? These are some of the mysteries we must learn to live with if we are to work with special children. We ask them to have faith, to hope, to love, to trust. Can we do less?

We have been asked occasionally: Don't you think your expectations are a little high for special children? Regis Duffy, commenting on the lack of religious commitment in our church communities today, quotes from John Gardner's *Grendel:*

> There is no conviction in the old priest's songs; there is only showmanship. No one in the Kingdom is convinced that the gods have life in them. The weak observe the rituals—take their hats off, put them on again, raise their arms, moan, intone, press their palms together—but no one harbors unreasonable expectations.[2]

The line "but no one harbors unreasonable expectations" may seem a harsh indictment of our religious rituals, but it is, nevertheless, a good reminder to ask ourselves some questions. Have we become so uncommitted, so reason-oriented, that we have lost faith that God can fulfill his promises, that the person who has faith can, indeed, move mountains, and that in weakness the power of Christ will be fulfilled? We have said that Jesus had a bias for the poor, the wounded, those in need of healing, those whom the world so often rejects. Can we doubt that he is as biased today as he ever was?

There is nothing wrong with having high expectations for our students as long as these are tempered by love and the willingness to accept our students' efforts as the gifts that they are. Although we cannot look into the future, we can certainly put our faith in the God who holds our future in his hands.

Notes

1. David Elkind, *Children and Adolescents,* N.Y., Oxford University Press, 1981.

2. Duffy, *op. cit.,* p. xi.

Part Two

Principles of Programming

Prologue

Y ou're a parent of a special child. As your child's brothers and sisters reluctantly prepare for religion class, your special child complains: "Why can't I go? I love God too."

You're a religion teacher. A friend with a physically disabled child complains: "Why don't they have a program for Susie? You know we don't know how long we'll have her with us, and we'd like her to receive Communion while she can, and maybe learn a little about her religion. We feel that's important."

You're a pastor. Every Sunday his parents bring Eddie to church and spend the hour trying to hold him still. Eddie's hyperactive, but his parents are determined. After all, he belongs too.

And so he does, and so do all the Susies and Eddies of this world in which there are about four hundred million disabled persons.[1] In the United States alone the handicapped make up 12.5% of the population.[2]

There is no reason why any child should be denied the opportunity for religious education. It is the Church's obligation to establish programs, therefore.[3] But don't wait around for someone else to do it. You may have a long wait. And after all, you are the Church.

Notes

1. *Pastoral Care and Catechesis of the Disabled,* Lumen Vitae, Volume 36, 1981. Brussels, Belgium.

2. *Special Religious Education,* Diocese of San Diego, California, 1981.

3. U.S. Catholic Conference, *Pastoral Statement of U.S. Catholic Bishops on Handicapped People,* Nov. 16, 1978.

4

Getting Started

This chapter will help you deal step by step with the process of setting up a parish program for special religious education. It discusses the practical problems involved in starting a center, including what to do with children with a diversity of handicaps and with parents who aren't sure if this is the right program for their children. The process is not difficult, but it takes time, so allow yourself at least six months for these preliminaries.

Step 1
Surveying the Possibilities

You've recognized the need for a special religious education center in your parish or church, and now you're ready to assess what kind of response you might get were such a program to be established. As you will surely be asked, now is the time to start thinking about the general outlines of your proposed program. (Reading Part I of this book should help you with that.) This will involve a decision as to who is to be included in the class.

Do all this before you seek permission, so that when the time comes to do so, you will have a concrete proposal prepared, the philosophy behind which you will be able to defend.

Assuming that you are either the parent of a special child or know the parent of a special child, it is time now to start a chain of inquiry going. Consult with the parents of the special children that you know. They will in turn give you the names of other parents to call. If these parents belong to a local concerned parents group, ask them to inquire at one of their meetings to see if there are perhaps other parents from a neighboring church or parish who might have an interest in such a center. You may also have a local association for retarded, handicapped, deaf or disabled persons in your vicinity. Contact them, and ask if they have ever had inquiries for such a program, or if they know of any existing programs in churches in the area. The diocesan religious education office might also have some useful information for you.

Although we acknowledge the promise of Jesus that wherever two or three are gathered in his name, he is there in the midst (Mt 18:20), and there is nothing wrong with a small group, it is, nevertheless, nice to have a slightly larger community than two or three. The children enjoy it better. So if you have only a few handicapped youngsters in your church or parish, contact your neighboring churches. Inquire whether they have ever had an interest in starting such a program and whether there are any special children in their communities. Let them know that you are surveying the situation locally and hope to start a center in which their youngsters could participate.

Step 2
Whom To Include

As you are collecting this information, you will no doubt be asked, "Well, whom is this program for? Is it just for the mentally handicapped? What about physically handicapped and learning disabled children?" As stated in the introduction to this book and in the National Catechetical Directory for Catholics, 1978 (no. 195), a handicapped person is anyone who has special needs which cannot be met in a regular classroom situation. This includes all sorts of disabilities both mental and physical. If this may seem rather straightforward, be forewarned. It's not that simple. One of the first problems you will encounter is the parents of special children who don't believe that their children can't manage in a regular religion program and don't want them placed with more severely brain-damaged children. Each of these cases will have to be handled individually and with compassion, remembering that the parents might be right. Some children in special education situations in schools do well in everyday religious education settings.

My general advice is that when the time comes, try to talk the director of religious education into letting these children try a regular classroom. If it doesn't work, they can always join your center at a later date.

Suppose, however, the DRE says no, or the child tries and it doesn't work, and the parents are still not sure they want their child in your program. If this is the case, invite the parents to sit in on a class or two with their child and see what goes on at your center. Encourage them to participate in one of your center's liturgies. Explain that you will be putting the children with similar handicaps together for small group sessions. Let the parents know that there may come a day when their child may be able to join a regular group, and that you will cooperate when the time comes to try it again. Assure them that you are always available to talk and that their child is always welcome in your center.

You might also explain to parents that most learning disabled or physically handicapped children (even those with higher I.Q.'s) would be happier in a class with other handicapped children, regardless of their disability. And there are advantages. For a change, the learning disabled children may have a chance to be among the smartest in the class, and the physically disabled will not feel as though everyone is looking at them, or that they are being patronized. It's nice to fit in somewhere until you're ready to take on the world. So gently suggest to parents that their children may need time to grow, and such a program as you envision might give their children a place to do so. Everyone needs a place to be comfortable, to belong: a place where an Eddie can move around during liturgy without embarrassing his parents or annoying others; a place where Eddie and Susie will be encouraged to participate in ways not open to them at a regular Sunday liturgy or in a regular classroom; a place where their handicaps will be taken into consideration in the lesson planning; a place where they will always have the individual attention they need.

An excellent addition to a special religious education program would be the pre-school children of your teachers and aides. Aside from the fact that it often solves a baby-sitting problem, such an arrangement is popular with the pre-schoolers and an advantage to the special students. At the age of four or five children still consider religion class a privilege, and they invariably interact naturally and sympathetically with their handicapped brothers and sisters. Their presence encourages the participation of special children, as they are little enough not to be considered a threat.

Step 3
Preparing and Presenting the Proposal

You've been talking to (other) parents. They're anxious to hear what you're planning. Hopefully, you've read Part I of this book and have been able to give them some broad outline of what you envision. You are now ready to give some thought to the proposal you wish to make to your governing body, be it the pastor, parish council or a group of elders. Part I has helped you to prepare the catechetical component of your program, but there are still some practical matters to be decided. Will your program be independent of the parish religious education program or will it be a part of it? Where will you meet? Who will finance you? Where will you get supplies? And who will coordinate your program?

There are, of course, many excellent existing programs which successfully solve these problems in a variety of ways, but if you are just beginning I would like to make some suggestions which in my experience have merit.

Your program should be part of the total parish religious education program and partake in the benefits of it. The children will be happier if they attend at the same time as their brothers and sisters and belong to the same overall program. In our parish brothers and sisters of children from outside our parish are invited to join our church's religious education program. This makes scheduling and transportation easier for the parents. If you pay the same fee as everyone else, or even if there is no fee, the supplies and resources of the parish program should be available to you. This is only just. However, as you may need some supplies that are specialized, and they may exceed the budget allotted to your program, you may need to find other resources. (For a discussion of this see Chapters 2 and 5.)

You will need a classroom with easy access for wheelchairs both to the outside and to the bathrooms. Other details of the classroom will depend on your size, structure and the participants. (For details see Chapter 5 on class structure.)

At the very least you will need a coordinator for your program who may double as the lead teacher. As most DRE's have little or no experience in special religious education, and your needs may be significantly different from those of the regular classes, your coordinator and your DRE may prefer your program to be administered separately. The

DRE should, however, be kept informed about all that is going on in your center and receive copies of liturgies, correspondence, etc. If it should be the case that the DRE has experience in special religious education, you may have your problem of finding a coordinator solved.

Your assisting teachers will benefit from the catechetical training programs available to other teachers in your parish and should be considered part of the total parish community of volunteer catechists.

With these things in mind, prepare to present your proposal to your governing body or pastor, noting that if the program is approved, you will have to advertise for teachers in the church bulletins.

Step 4
Finding a Coordinator

You've been given the green light, and if it seems expedient, and you haven't already done this, now is the time to talk with the parish DRE about the needs of your envisioned center. Ask the DRE for the names of people who might be willing to volunteer to help with your program: in particular for the name of someone who might be qualified to coordinate the program. (For qualifications see Chapter 5.) With any luck in the process of assessing your needs, you will have already come upon some helpers.

Place in your parish bulletin and in those of other interested churches a notice such as the following:

> St. Mary's Church in New Monmouth is opening a center for the religious education of developmentally impaired children and youth. All children with mental, physical, emotional or learning handicaps are welcome. Teachers and aides will be needed to staff the program. We need your help. Come join us for an information evening _____night at _____o'clock in _____. For information call _____at _____.
>
> (your name)   (your phone number)

Explain to those who attend what you have in mind, and the various ways volunteers could help. (Chapter 5 should help you with this.) Promise those who feel unqualified that you will provide a workshop or training session to help them. (See Appendix III.) If possible bring

in someone with experience in special religious education to share some
of his or her experience and expertise. Your diocesan office may be able
to help you locate such a person.

Now, if you are not to be the coordinator, you can retire and leave
Step 5 to the coordinator.

Step 5
Researching Curriculum Resources

As detailed in Chapter 5, the coordinator and/or lead teacher has
many responsibilities, but, at this time, to get started he or she will have
to concentrate on locating curriculum materials, training teachers and
preparing for registration.

An annotated bibliography appended to this book may help with
curriculum materials. This bibliography contains only those materials
we have used and found satisfactory. There are no doubt other good
sources with which we are not familiar. As no set of lesson plans will
solve all your needs indefinitely, Chapters 6 and 7 will tell you how to
prepare your own year plan and lesson plans. You may find that using
these guidelines and incorporating into them some of the lesson plans
in the bibliography will give you the program that you want. It's a bit
of work initially, but worth the results as it gives you leeway for infinite
variations over the years. Otherwise after a few years you've used up
all the available lesson plans, have the same children in your class, and
don't know what to do next.

After you've ordered curriculum materials, make sure you own or
have access to books of ditto masters (they cover all topics), a flannel
board and figures (two or three boards if you have a large class), fat
crayons for uncoordinated little fingers and thin crayons for others,
magic markers, paper, clay, washable paint, scissors, paste, tape, record player or tape deck with records and tapes, rhythm instruments
(nice for children who can't sing), poster board and whatever else you
might be inclined to use. (See bibliography for purchase reference.)

You've picked the day and the time for registration. Make it three
or four weeks before you're ready to begin so that you have time afterward to plan your program around the students. Once you have an
established program this will not be as important, as you will probably
only get two or three new students each year.

Put announcements in your parish and local churches' bulletins.

Remember that some parishes only put their bulletins out once a month, so leave plenty of time for this. If you cannot make use of the bulletins, make eye-catching posters for the bulletin boards.

Place announcements in your local and diocesan papers and in regional newsletters for the handicapped. Ask those parents you know to spread the word. Although we do all this publicity every year and it is necessary, it is our experience that most of our students are referred to us by word of mouth. So if you don't get a large response the first day of registration, be patient. The word will spread.

On registration day ask the parents to bring their children so that you can take a moment to get acquainted, get a look at who your students are going to be, and let the children know how excited you are to have them in your class this year.

At registration time it is a good idea to have the parents fill out a registration card similar to the one in this chapter. The questions asked will help you in your endeavors as well as providing a permanent record card for each child. Children should not need to reregister from year to year, and parents should be assured that only you and your teachers will have access to the record card.

Now you're ready to begin and it's time to read the next three chapters. If you are a coordinator, make sure your teachers read at least Part I and Chapter 7. The tips in Chapter 5 may also be of interest to them.

SPECIAL EDUCATION

PERMANENT RECORD CARD

PERSONAL INFORMATION

NAME _____ M.A. _____ I.Q. _____ DATE OF BIRTH _____ PHONE _____

ADDRESS _____ RELIGIOUS AFFILIATION _____ PARISH _____

_____

FATHER'S NAME _____ ADDRESS _____ OCCUPATION _____

FATHER'S RELIGION _____ PHONE _____

MOTHER'S NAME _____ ADDRESS _____ OCCUPATION _____

MOTHER'S RELIGION _____ PHONE _____

GUARDIAN'S NAME _____ ADDRESS _____ OCCUPATION _____

GUARDIAN'S RELIGION _____ PHONE _____

IN CASE OF EMERGENCY CALL _____ PHONE _____

TYPE OR CAUSE OF IMPAIRMENT IF KNOWN _____

ADDITIONAL HANDICAPS (EXPLAIN) _____

_____

CHILDREN IN FAMILY

CHILD	DATE OF BIRTH	CHILD	DATE OF BIRTH

RECORD OF RELIGIOUS FORMATION

DATE OF BAPTISM _____ CHURCH _____ PLACE _____

DATE OF CONFIRMATION _____ CHURCH _____ PLACE _____

DATE OF RECEPTION OF HOLY EUCHARIST _____ CHURCH _____ PLACE _____

RECEPTION OF ADDITIONAL SACRAMENTS: _____

SACRAMENT _____ DATE _____ CHURCH _____ PLACE _____

SACRAMENT _____ DATE _____ CHURCH _____ PLACE _____

5

Of Students, Teachers and Structure

Introducing the Special Child

People on occasion say to me, "How can you teach these children? It must be so difficult? Isn't it depressing? I could never do that." What they don't usually say, but are so often thinking, is, "They look so strange. I'm afraid of them. They repulse me, and so I'm sure I could never learn to love and teach them."

My answer to all inquiries is always, "Yes, you could, and you'd love it." All you need is a little time and a willing heart. Working with special children is a love feast, a communion, a shared ministry. If there is anywhere in this world where you can be sure to meet God, it is in a ministry with the handicapped. But, as with all relationships, love grows as you get to know each other, and if you are not willing to extend yourself, to give it a try, you will be denying yourself both a great opportunity to grow in the love of Christ and a great privilege.

Once you fall in love with special children (and this invariably happens as you get to know them), it becomes increasingly difficult to stay consciously aware of their handicaps. This is not to say that you no longer notice that the young people with whom you work are blind, brain-damaged, etc., but that their handicaps no longer determine your relationship with them, and you tend to forget about them. As you begin to know the child behind the face and body, you become aware of that child's special graces, the reflection of God in his or her eyes, and what seemed ugly becomes beautiful. Suddenly, you are aware that despite their appearances and/or their handicaps, these children have the same feelings, the same reactions, the same emotional moods and needs of all children their age. As one priest who works with the handicapped once said to me, "When you think of the great distance between God and us, the distance between us and our handicapped brothers and sisters no longer seems so great."[1]

For a while, I worried that this inability to focus on their handicaps, might be a disadvantage to me as their teacher. Perhaps it would prevent me from making the necessary allowances in my teaching methods. Perhaps my expectations would be beyond their abilities. Instead I discovered that the children responded and learned best when they were loved and treated like any other child or youth of the same age. In a loving atmosphere they responded to high expectations as both a challenge and a compliment. What I had to remember was not to get too worried about their ability to verbalize what they had learned and to simply accept whatever their achievements might be with praise, trusting that God would complete in them the work that I felt I had so inadequately begun.

In truth, Christian educators of special children know that it is they who are being gifted, they who are being transformed, and that can only be an occasion of joy.

> *Love has no room for fear; rather, perfect love casts out all fear (1 Jn 4:18).*

No people are more loving and affectionate, more responsive to attention and affirmation, than special children. An abrasive or defensive attitude on the part of a special child is rare, but when it does happen one must be aware of the fear of rejection (perhaps the result of rejection at home) that has caused such an attitude. Such children need time to become comfortable and secure in your presence and group. They need to be reassured of their lovableness, and this is not always easy, as they can work hard at being defiant and testing. Patience on the part of their teachers and parents is important, for these children need time to grow. If they are adolescents, one must remember that they will go through the same adolescent crises of all youth. If they are younger, they may just be beginning to notice that they can't keep up or compete with other children their age. The children in the neighborhood are calling them "retard" and they ride special busses to school. Under these circumstances it is not surprising that they develop frustration and anger and show signs of rebellion.

Observing this can be heartbreaking because of one's inability to control the situation. Nevertheless, it can provide us with a unique illustration of our Christian belief in the transforming power of love, for the long-term reward for patience and love tempered by firmness in these crises is usually a growth in trust and an attitudinal change, after which things start to improve all around. As is so often the case in parenting and teaching, perseverance, faith and love are the keys.

Class Structure

As the structure of a program will determine the functions of the participants, I would like to preface a discussion of the functions and responsibilities of the teaching team with a brief description of the program structure that we here at St. Mary's have found most effective. This is not intended to be the definitive word on the subject, but a model, a place to begin for those interested in opening a new center as well as a measure of evaluation for established centers. While it is intended primarily for church school or CCD type settings, the material could easily be adapted for use in institutions and schools.

After much experimentation and observation we have settled on the following class structure as being most effective for us. You might try variations to suit your circumstances. If the class size is under 15–20, one main room with perhaps another room for small group work should be sufficient. A classroom with movable desks and chairs and a chalkboard is perhaps easiest to adapt for your needs (or perhaps some sort of all-purpose room with tables and chalkboard). You will need enough room to set up a Scripture center, make a circle for prayer and storytelling times, and form into small groups for arts and crafts and discussion periods. As you will have children of all sizes in your class, and it may prove difficult to get a classroom with different size chairs and tables or desks, try for a fourth or fifth grade classroom with perhaps a table for which you can bring in some small chairs for the little ones. Good lighting is essential, both for the cheerful atmosphere it provides and because many handicapped children have eye coordination problems.

If your class meets weekly, 1 to 1½ hours maximum is a good length. Special children need a variety of activities and a chance to move around and stretch periodically as many have a limited attention span. Unless you have children consistently coming in late, or you like to do a lot of extra singing and art work, most lesson plans can be completed in an hour. Allocate sport and social activities to another time or day.

Plan to meet as a group for the first half hour. Arrive early to collect supplies and set up the room. Have music playing as a welcome.

As the students come in, teachers and aides can distribute early bird specials. (For details on lesson planning see Chapter 7.) When the class is assembled the lead teacher will introduce the theme for the day followed by the related Scripture reference, prayer or prayer service, music and singing. (The latter could be under the direction of either the lead teacher or a music coordinator.) Time allotted for each of these activities will vary with the lesson plan, but, considering the children's limited attention span, a half-hour should be enough.

After the first half-hour, break your group into smaller groups which meet at different ends of the room or in as many other rooms as you have available. Remember, special children are easily distracted, so the more you can spread out your groups the better. Plan to have the teachers' backs to the walls and the students facing the teachers. This will help focus attention on the teacher and avoid distractions from other corners of the room.

The composition of these sub-groups will be determined by age, handicap, and content matter. There may be a First Holy Communion group, a confirmation group, a group studying reconciliation, a young adult group composed of more severely handicapped youth and a second one composed of learning disabled youth. If you have deaf children they may benefit from being in a group with a teacher with some experience in sign or lip reading. However, if there is only one deaf child, include him or her in a regular group, making sure that his or her seat faces you directly as you speak and that you look at him or her when you speak.

Try never to put older children with little ones. Regardless of their handicaps it is humiliating for older children. If older children are new in your group and just now preparing for Holy Communion as are the little ones, it is preferable to place them in an older group and have aides work with them on Communion material.

Each sub-group should be headed by a teacher assisted by as many aides as needed for the children in the group. Hyperactive children, children with damaged muscle-control, deaf or blind children and severely brain-damaged children will need an aide just for them. Under this arrangement, if a child is tired, restless, or disruptive, the aide can take him or her for a walk, for a drink or into another room to listen to a record and talk about the lesson in quiet. In these small groups the theme for the day (introduced earlier by the lead teacher) is developed with an eye toward the learning level of the students involved. The art or drama activity geared to the abilities of the students involved and to the lesson theme should be part of this last half hour.

If you have more than twenty children involved you might consider dividing the class into older and younger students and running two totally separate classrooms following the above format. If you have a large amount of slightly learning disabled children, they might form a separate class. You could still be in neighboring classrooms and share monthly liturgies, social and sport events and an occasional classroom get-together. You would then need a second lead teacher and more room, but it would be a worthwhile endeavor, for while too few students in a group is no fun for the students and inhibits community building, too many precludes total student participation and puts serious limitations on the lead teacher. As your program grows, and those who have been with you as children become young adults, moving them into a separate classroom with a new teacher and a more grown-up program also has its advantages. Older children often prefer more grown-up music, drama and art activities, and in a smaller and quieter group they will mature in their responses to prayer meditations and paraliturgies.

DEVELOPING A TEAM

A religious education center, if it hopes to be a community in Christ, needs to be the work of shared ministry. Teachers, aides, students, parents, siblings, friends, minister or priest, all fulfill, though some more consciously than others, a specific function in your program.

Once the structure of the program has been determined, you can decide who will fill what role(s), and what other kind of help is needed. This will vary according to the number of students involved and the nature of their handicaps. Most likely you will start small with a coordinator and a few teachers filling several roles, but as you grow and discover the talents of those involved in the program and the talent still needed, it would be advisable to have, at the very least, a coordinator who may or may not double as lead teacher, several assistant teachers, some adult and/or teenage aides and several people, perhaps parents, willing to help with extra-curricular activities. Among your teachers and aides you will need a coordinator for arts and crafts, music, and liturgy. Depending on your situation one person may fill two or three of these roles. That is not problematic as long as it does not lead to the neglect of any one of these components, since they are all essential to developing a vibrant ministry.

The Coordinator

If you are in a church or parish setting, chances are that the co-ordinator or director of your program will also be the lead teacher in charge of planning the total program for the year. In fact, this may be preferable, since no one should coordinate such a program who has not had experience in the religious education of special children. While the coordinator/lead teacher does not have to be a trained special education teacher (remember the number one requirement is to be a great lover), some background in catechetics, theology and/or perhaps developmental psychology would be useful and could be shared in meetings and workshops with assisting teachers who do not have this background.

If it is impossible to find a person with this background, perhaps a parent of an adult handicapped child with some background in catechesis could with the help of a book such as this fill the role. However, in either case the coordinator/lead catechist should make some attempt at continuing education in this field and should encourage assisting teachers to do so also. This could be in the form of reading (see bibliography), a course at a seminary or community college, workshops (inquire at your regional religious education office), and/or visitations to established centers.

The responsibilities of the coordinator/lead catechist are to meet with and instruct the assistant teachers and aides, research curriculum materials, plan the program for the year and direct the first half hour of classtime, delegate responsibilities and thereafter oversee their execution, prepare the budget and yearly financial report for the pastor or parish council, keep contact with parents encouraging their involvement, and keep the files containing the records of the students and the history of the center.

Copies should be kept of all letters mailed to parents or others, all year plans, all liturgical programs, as well as records of the students' histories and sacramental involvement. These cards are important for the teachers' understanding of their students and should be made available to the teachers when planning their classes.

The planning of the program for the year (details of which are in Chapter 6) can be done by either the coordinator/lead catechist alone or with the other teachers, depending on the interest, expertise and available time of the assisting teachers. At the very least a teachers' meeting at which the plan for the year is reviewed in dialogue is essential.

If there is no budget for your center from parish resources, an annual fee can be charged. Charge the same fee that regular CCD students pay, but take into consideration the financial situation of the families. The fee could be considered voluntary, or a donation. Charitable organizations such as the Knights of Columbus and the Elks could be contacted for a donation to your budget. Don't be afraid to ask local tradespeople for special prices for your supplies, and PTA's, etc., for donations of crayons, paper and leftover craft materials. As ideally you should be part of your church's total religious education program, its supplies should also be at your disposal.

A good leader delegates responsibility and thereby develops new leadership. Hopefully, as time goes by, others in the program can assume some of the initial responsibilities of the coordinator. At the opening meeting with new teachers, find out what roles the teachers see themselves as filling most easily, where their interests lie, what they would like to do. Try different arrangements for a while until everyone begins to appreciate what works best. Perhaps after the first half year or year, ask one teacher to take charge of all the arts and crafts activities, coordinating them to the lesson plans. You may even have a talented teenager willing to do this. If you find no one with particular musical talent, check the folk group in your church for a possible guitar player or just use records and tapes. Unless you have weekly access to an organ, piano or guitar player, records and tapes are the best, as they can be transported almost anywhere you may want to sing (e.g., church, nursing home, party, etc.).

Assistant Teachers

Your core team in charge of catechesis consists of the coordinator/lead teacher and your assistant teachers. As stated previously in this chapter the assisting teachers are responsible for developing the theme for the day in the small group sessions. As there are few detailed teacher's manuals for special religious education it is highly advisable that these teachers have some sort of catechetical training. These training sessions need not be exclusively geared for special religious education teachers, as to some extent the same background is pertinent for all

Christian educators. In addition, a workshop explicitly on teaching special religious education should be offered at least once a year and occasional meetings held to discuss the progress of the program and to build teacher community.

It is the responsibility of the small group teachers to get to know the students in their groups more intimately and to keep contact with the parents. Often there are personal and family crises which will only become apparent to someone who works with students in a small group. These crises should be brought to the attention of the coordinator and other teachers to assess what, if any, assistance could be offered.

Aides

Teenagers and adults with no time to prepare lesson plans, but with a little love to spare and an hour a week to give to this service, make excellent aides. Many of our best teachers were former aides, and many of our teenage aides have gone on to college to major in special education.

Teenagers and young adults may also be interested in assisting with a weekly bowling or basketball program, helping out at social affairs and participating in and chaperoning outings and community service projects. Grandmother and grandfather aides bring the gifts of time, love, understanding and wisdom to students of all ages who need another adult guarantor or maybe just a lap to sit on and someone to listen to their problems.

Parents

Many parents of special children are so burdened already that they have little time to give to our programs and are happy just to participate in monthly worship services and social affairs. Others may feel unqualified for such a ministry. They should be encouraged to participate and be reassured that their experience and love is the most valuable gift they could bring to a center.

If parents wish to teach, it is generally advisable not to place them in the same small group as their children.

Other parents may be willing to run social or sporting events, chaperone outings, or even bake or shop for supplies for you. At the initial parents' meeting, let parents know how they can help. Suggest that they come and observe a class from time to time, and find time to sit and have a cup of coffee with them when they do. As the lead teacher is usually free the second half hour of class time, this time could be used to consult with parents.

Minister or Priest

Hopefully, one of your parish ministers or priests, if not involved in your program on a weekly basis, will be available for monthly liturgies and an occasional surprise visit to the classroom. As a representative of the larger church community, their presence is a sign both of their personal caring and interest in your center and of the support of the larger community.

Friends

A friend to your center is generally anyone who comes in the door. Welcome into your programs anyone who knocks or, as the story goes, you may miss the Christ Child when he comes. With a little help from the Lord you will find a place for whoever knocks, and eventually, you will find out what gift such persons have brought with them.

COMMANDMENTS AND TIPS FOR TEACHING
AND REACHING SPECIAL CHILDREN

He who loves his brother abides in the light, and in it there is no cause for stumbling (1 Jn 2:10).

As John has said (Jn 13:34) and Paul has made so beautifully clear in his letter to the Corinthians (1 Cor 13), there is but one commandment, one way—the way of love. All other commandments, all other tips, all training, all gifts, are useless unless anchored in love. This is not, of course, a love without discipline, but a demanding love that sees the image of God in each student and thereby each student's infinite human value and potential.

Henri Bissonier, the father of catechetics for the handicapped, describes the characteristics of this love as follows:

1. True love is esteem for the person one loves.

2. Love is characterized by seeking the good of the one loved.
3. True love does not exclude but demands competence.
4. Love is synonomous with the gift of self to the "other."
5. Love constitutes a real way of knowing.[2]

Should this emphasis on love seem particularly redundant to readers, it is important to remember that when teaching the handicapped "esteem and love are preliminary conditions for all effective action."[3] It may be only through your love that some may know God. The commandment to love then is not hard to understand, it is just sometimes hard to do.[4]

In addition to the catechetical "tips" liberally spread throughout this book, especially in Chapter 2, I shall list a few here. They are only intended to supplement my comments in Part I. Almost every book of lesson plans is prefaced with similar suggestions. I add these to the many, for I know it is comforting for new teachers to have such a list. I would, however, not want thereby to put a limitation on anyone's creativity, imagination or desire to try something new or to do it differently. There are many ways of achieving similar goals, and what works with one child for one teacher may not work for or with another. This is particularly true for handicapped children. When anchored in the love of Christ, it is perfectly possible that there are as many undreamed of suggestions and solutions as there are listed below and elsewhere in this book.

1. Use repetition. Special children thrive on repetition, so present the same concept or idea in a variety of ways, using a variety of media. Singing the same songs week after week is not boring for special children, but rather it enables them to participate more comfortably.
2. Limit yourself to one theme a week so as to avoid confusion. Let the weekly themes flow into each other in logical sequence. (See Chapters 6 and 7.) Use concrete rather than abstract examples to illustrate your themes, relating these to your children's lives.
3. Conduct your class in dialogue with the students, always emphasizing the value of students' contributions to the discussion. (See Chapters 2 and 7.)
4. Speak in a moderate voice, but firmly, letting the children know

you expect them to be attentive. Avoid shouting and raising your voice. An ordered atmosphere gives the children security.

5. Call only on those who raise their hands, while encouraging all to do so through the use of affirmation techniques. (See Chapter 2.) The exception to this is if you are going around the room sharing experiences and opinions. As there is, in such circumstances, no right or wrong or any particular knowledge necessary to answer, don't in this case omit anyone when you call on the children.

6. Give children time to answer, and affirm what they are saying. "Encourage them to express themselves through gesture or sign. With a speech-impaired child whom you can't understand, develop non-committal responses—'Is that so? Oh?' And encourage a motor response."[5] Listen with your eyes as well as with your ears. Body language will often tell you what cannot be said.[6]

7. Be flexible. If it looks as though your lesson is going to be a flop and/or everyone is getting restless and inattentive, be prepared to drop the whole thing and do something else. Instead, have a rap session; play a game; sing some favorite songs.

8. Have a sense of humor and don't take yourself too seriously. Laughter can be redeeming and the children love to have a good laugh, especially on occasion at the teacher's expense. Role playing can be excellent for a laugh.

9. Touch your students. Most special children need this physical contact. "You can tell them that God loves them; you can tell them that you love them. But, unless you reach out and touch them lovingly—a hug, a pat, a kiss—many will not believe or comprehend."[7]

10. "Do not add to the problems of your students by allowing them to do and say whatever they please."[8] Each class situation and each student is different, so it is impossible to give a comprehensive directive about discipline, but, in general, let the children know you expect good behavior of them and remember that most of them are capable of it. You will develop insight into this as time goes on, but it behooves you to begin with that "demanding love."

11. If a child is consistently disrupting a class for whatever reason, have an aide take him or her to another room, for a drink of water or for a walk. Try consistently to give this child things to do so that he or she will have less time to disrupt. None of these solutions need appear to be a punishment. If things do not improve, discuss

the situation with the parents for suggestions. There may be an easy solution to the problem and there may not, but in either case let the parents know that you care and are willing to keep trying. For some children you may simply be providing another caring environment, but that may have more value for that child and parents than you can imagine.

12. Don't get discouraged. The children will sense it and feel that it is their fault. Try to stay enthusiastic and/or stick with topics you're enthusiastic about. Enthusiasm is catching also.

13. Leave something for God to do. God is your best resource.

Notes

1. William Bohnsack, pastor, St. Leo the Great Church, Lincroft, N.J.

2. Henri Bissonier, *op. cit.,* p. 13.

3. *Ibid.,* p. 14.

4. John L. McKenzie, *What the Bible Says About the Problems of Contemporary Life,* Thomas More Association, Chicago, Illinois, 1983, in "Source."

5. *Special Religious Education, Catechist Formation and Resource Book,* pamphlet by Sister Kathryn Jennings, O.S.B. and Ms. Betty Britschgi for the Diocese of San Diego, 1981, p. 15.

6. Dorothy Clark, Jane Dahl, Lois Gonzenback, *Teach Me, Please Teach Me,* David C. Cook Publishing Co. Elgin, Ill., 1974, p. 13.

7. *Ibid.,* p. 13.

8. *Ibid.,* pp. 13–14.

6

Preparing a Plan for the Year

Preparing a plan for the year is an undertaking that is relatively simple when first starting a center, but becomes progressively more difficult as the years go by, your center grows, and you become ever more aware of the limited resources available. Nevertheless, with a little ingenuity you can put together an infinite variety of programs whose scope will depend on the make-up of your class, your purpose and the amount of time you have available.

What is absolutely essential is that you *have* a plan for the year, and that you do not nonchalantly go from week to week or even month to month without an overall scheme. Lessons must have purposeful sequence related to what you are trying to achieve and how you best hope to achieve that. (See Part I.)

In addition to lessons a plan for the year will necessitate scheduling liturgies, community service projects and social and sport events. This will involve taking a good look at the budget and deciding what is financially feasible. It will also necessitate a decision as to who is willing to take responsibility for what activities.

At the end of each year, promptly after closing the center for the summer, all teachers should meet for an evaluation of the past year's program, bringing to this meeting also suggestions for improving the program in the following year.

Over the summer the coordinator can take some time studying these suggestions, ordering and studying new materials and consulting with individual teachers as to what direction they feel their participation in the program could take in the following year. A plan for the coming year can then be drawn up.

Resources

In drawing up your plan your use of the rather limited resources available will depend on what you are trying to accomplish. Some of the existing lesson plans are predominantly theologically (sacramentally) and ethically (morally) oriented. These call for much repetition and the memorization of concepts. Because of their ethical-theological thrust and the time element involved, their use of Scripture and storytelling is, unfortunately, limited. Other sources which are more scripturally oriented often fail to link the Scripture lesson to the student's life situation. Many are theologically very out-of-date or inappropriate for special children. Still other resources simply present groups of lesson plans on a variety of topics, to be used as you see fit. Some of the latter are excellent; most can be adapted for your use.

At least one excellent program of which I am aware roughly follows the liturgical calendar and does a good job on balancing the use of Scripture and theology.[1] Unfortunately, this is only a two year Communion program, intended for young children.

Many centers use pre-school and primary materials from major publishers and adapt these for special children. This can be successfully done provided you have experience in the field of catechetics with special children. But beware—older children using books with pictures of young children in them often find this insulting. Also older children, though slow learners, do not think like little ones. Thus, the older the children in your group, the more difficult this type of adaptation will be. A second difficulty is that even first grade students' manuals call for reading and writing beyond the ability of most special children of the same age. Thus, even though you may be able to adapt the lessons from the teachers' manuals, in most cases the students' manuals cannot be used.

In fact, there are practically no students' manuals available for special religious education. The best substitute you can provide is a folder or a notebook for each child to which you add each week. A good supply of religious ditto (spirit) masters[2] plus those ditto masters you make yourself can help in developing material for such a folder.

Among the best resources for teachers are the more philosophically oriented works on special people and special religious education by the French pioneers in the field, Henri Bissonier and Jean Vanier. (See annotated bibliography.) These do not contain lesson plans per se, but give ample tips on how to understand, work with and help special people, plus ideas on how to put a lesson plan together.

Thus, despite the drawbacks of much of the available material, if you survey it, you will find many good, adaptable ideas. The first thing to do is to plan an overall scheme and then decide what of the available material fits your plan.

Planning the Year

Most programs run from September to May and include between twenty and thirty classes. On a sheet of paper list your class days in conjunction with your students' school calendars. Coordinate your holidays with theirs. Your calendar should hopefully also coincide with the calendar of your total parish religious education program. As registration has been completed earlier your opening day can be reserved for getting to know each other's activities for parents and children and perhaps a liturgy and family social. Mark in the class days before Christmas and Easter for special celebrations. Plan when you are going to have your monthly liturgies and what will be their themes. These themes should be coordinated with your lesson plan sequence. Write in any other special events which you might be celebrating that year, such as First Holy Communion, confirmation and communal penance. Confirm these dates with your priest or minister. By the time you have done all this you will probably have room left for between fifteen and twenty lessons.

A decision now has to be made as to the overall scheme for the year, and for this I would recommend what I call a Trinitarian scheme. For Catholics this would be in keeping with the directives of the National Catechetical Directory (n. 47) and roughly synchronized with the liturgical year. In such a scheme our relationship with God the Father is the subject of lessons from September until Advent. From Advent until Easter our relationship with Jesus, God's Son, is studied, using stories from Jesus' life and ours. And from Easter until the end of the year the lessons dwell on the action of the Spirit in our lives and in the lives of the first apostles.

A scheme such as this allows for a wide variety of lesson plans year after year as well as concentration year after year on the principal truths and moments of celebration of our faith. No year should go by without a discussion of both the meaning of the birth of Jesus and of his passion, or without a discussion of the wonder of creation and the action of the Spirit in our lives. First Holy Communion and confirmation celebrated in the time between Easter and Pentecost would be particularly appropriate, as would a communal penance service during Lent. As the number of annual lessons on God, Jesus and the Holy Spirit is limited, each year can see the inclusion of different stories and different aspects of our relationships with them.

A good guide to deciding the order of the themes to be used each week could be the liturgical calendar which runs in a three year cycle.[3] While not every week provides a Scripture reading which you can use (some are just too difficult for children and some won't fit your scheme), usually in the time between Advent and Easter one out of the three Sunday readings can be used. Study the readings as you develop your plan and see how they might fit in. If between September and Thanksgiving you find (as one does in Cycle C) the Gospel on the healing of the ten lepers (Lk 17:11), you could plan your lesson on thanking God for that week and work your lesson sequence around it.

As I have said earlier, children and youth are pleased if they find themselves familiar with the readings at Sunday liturgy, and they become, thereby, more attentive and involved. Thus, any effort expended in making these readings familiar to children is worthwhile as it will in the long run help to integrate them into the larger Christian community. While you do not want to depart from or disrupt your planned sequence, there are many times when, if looked at in advance, you can arrange your sequence to accommodate both your purpose and a Sunday Scripture reading.

If you have a group of older children doing a weekly Bible study, this works out particularly well as their teacher will most likely be using the lectionary as a guide.

With children preparing for sacramental initiation this system also works out well as, on the whole, the Scripture themes from Christmas to Pentecost develop along lines appropriate for Communion and confirmation study. You should sometime before First Communion, preferably just before Easter, include (this may necessitate substituting for the Sunday readings) lessons on the wedding feast at Cana (Jn 2:1–12) and the multiplication of the loaves and fishes (Mt 14:13–21; 15:32–38; Mk 6:32–44; Lk 9:10–17; Jn 6:1–13). These lessons could culminate in a discussion and/or dramatization of the Last Supper. Similarly, preparation for confirmation should be preceded by lessons discussing the action of the Spirit in our lives. Thus the best time for both Communion and confirmation is sometime in the spring after Easter. If you cannot arrange for this, plan the sequence for the Easter season anyway and review it briefly before the celebration.

As this overall scheme is appropriate for all ages, small group teachers can develop the various themes according to the needs and abilities of their students. Any topic which a particular teacher might feel important to include can usually be incorporated into this plan at some time during the year.

Admittedly, this does not allow for a lengthy or detailed study of any one topic during any given year. Instead, almost all topics are repeated year after year. It is my opinion, having tried it both ways, that with special children the above plan simply works better than a year's concentration on one or two theological points or on preparation exclusively for one sacrament. It holds the children's interest and provides for repetition on a yearly basis of the essential concepts and truths of our faith. On a weekly basis, when developed in conjunction with the methodological understanding of Part I, such a scheme fits the purpose of our religious educating, for it provides the children with a means of listening to God and to Jesus, with a way of understanding the good news and what it means in their lives. It allows for learning through storytelling which is particularly effective with special children, and it is adaptable for all ages and all learning levels.

Most of the lesson plans available have any number of lessons which can fit into or be adapted to this scheme. For those lessons you wish to teach for which you have no model you can develop your own lesson plan using the guidelines recommended in Chapter 7. In the Appendix of this book you will find some year plans which we have used and with which we have been pleased.

Using the Plan

Once you have drawn up your year's plan, it is time to sit down individually with your assisting teachers and discuss how they are going to develop the weekly themes in their small groups. All teachers should have copies of the year's plan with spaces left blank for them to note how they plan to treat each theme and what medium (art, drama, etc.) they will use.

At the opening meeting you might also give copies to parents so that they will know what is going on in class and possibly follow up at home.

Planning for Two or More Groups

If your group is over fifteen or twenty persons, and you are running two totally separate classes, one of older and one of younger students, you may want to plan differently. (For a discussion of class structure see Chapter 5.) As you can now have two plans, one specifically for younger and one for older children, you may in each instance be able to use some material that you could not have used if all students were together in one classroom. For instance, songs with motions such as *If I Were a Butterfly*[4] are only for young children. Older children feel silly and object to the motions and lyrics while younger ones love them. A discussion of symbols of our faith (fire, water, wind, light) related to sacrament can be successfully done with older children while little ones do better studying sacraments through drama and storytelling. Also older children can be reminded that they are growing up and that you expect more of them; that you will provide them with more grown-up challenges. Having said this, be sure to do so. In addition to intellectual challenges, they might now participate in projects using hammers, nails, oil paints, etc. They will enjoy this, and if these projects are purposefully designed, they will learn thereby.

In Conclusion

Whatever you do, your first year will be experimental, and you should not get discouraged if the results are not as you had envisioned them. It takes time to get the feel of what works best in each particular situation. As the year progresses, it is worthwhile to make notes on how you can improve your program or particular sections of it the following year. More teachers and aides can be added as you need them, and new resources are continually coming on the market. These should be appraised and tried if they seem promising.

Eventually you will find the format most suitable for your center. Then the only danger is that you might fail to continue to evaluate and upgrade your program in subsequent years. This is an easy pitfall to encounter, but then it is also an easy one to avoid.

Notes

1. Carol Podlasek, *Gift,* Winston Press, 1976.
2. *Spirit Masters* are available from a variety of sources. Most re-

cently we have used those from Arena Lettres, 8 Lincoln Place, Box
219, Waldwick, N.J. 07463.

   3. Sunday lectionaries with the A, B, and C, Cycle readings can
be purchased at your local religious book stores.

   4. From *Hi God II* by Carey Landry, published by North American Liturgy Resources, Phoenix, Arizona, 1975.

7

Preparing a Lesson Plan

People are more willing to listen to witnesses than to teachers, and if they listen to teachers at all, it is because they are witnesses (Paul VI).

Prayer and preparation—you can't do one without the other. They are the essential prerequisites for every lesson plan, to being a good witness in the classroom. Prayerful meditation on your students' needs and lives in relation to what you want to communicate ensures your teaching for their benefit, not your own. Petitioning the Holy Spirit to speak through you, to allow you to touch the hearts of your students, will result in your achieving goals you had not thought possible.

And then there's preparation, for which there is also no substitute. If you are a weekly volunteer and new to this, a minimum of an hour to an hour and a half of planning time should be set aside. You may need more. This preparation should be done at least two to three days in advance of the day you plan to present your lesson so that you will have time to collect art supplies or other media, run off spirit masters, practice your flannel board presentation, and so forth. If you are planning a liturgy, begin that planning at least two to three weeks prior to the day you have set so that the students can help in the preparations and those doing the readings can take them home to practice. Additional preparation time may be necessary for typing and running off programs, etc. The main thing is to *plan in advance* so that when the unexpected happens, you will have time to cope with it. One of the most important qualities of a good teacher is dependability,[1] and the only way to ensure your own dependability is to plan in advance.

On the day of your class try to arrive at least twenty to thirty minutes early so that you have ample time to arrange the classroom, collect supplies, greet early arrivals, delegate chores and communicate with parents who may wish to speak with you. As soon as you arrive put music on your tape recorder or record player and turn on lights so as to prepare a cheerful and welcoming atmosphere. Ask assistants to be at least ten minutes early so that they can help you greet people and get the children started on their early bird specials.

Every lesson should have six ingredients: (1) early bird specials; (2) presentation of the theme; (3) Scripture; (4) prayer; (5) music; (6) arts and crafts and/or drama. Try not to neglect any of these components no matter how briefly you use them. A variety of media and activities plus active participation is the most effective way of learning for special children. While these components need not be presented in the above order, they must complement and supplement each other. In other words, the prayer, the Scripture, the art and drama and the music, whenever possible, should reflect and flow out of the theme of the day.

Early Bird Specials

One of the problems we have not succeeded in solving is how to get parents to bring their children on time. Regardless of what ingenious schemes we have devised, there are always a few students who arrive fifteen minutes early, and a few more who straggle in ten minutes late. While one cannot delay starting the class for the stragglers, neither should one punish the early birds by telling them to sit quietly and wait for class to begin. Sitting quietly is quite difficult for most special children, and running around the classroom only increases their restlessness and makes them difficult to quiet down later on. Thus it would be expedient to have on hand a box of early bird specials: activities which the children can begin as soon as they come in the classroom—perhaps a picture to color, a puzzle, chalk (if they may write on the board), etc. Preferably the activity should be something simple and not too messy, and one that can be put away quickly when the class is ready to begin. (It might even be a project they can finish later on in their small groups.) Aides can supervise these activities, plus the putting on and off of coats, so that the teachers are free to speak to parents and set up their presentations.

The Presentation

The presentation introduces the theme of the day. Regardless of what media you use, it should be developed in dialogue with your students and related in some concrete manner to their life experience. This holds true either if you are the lead teacher and presenting the theme only briefly, or if you are a small group teacher going into more detail. The one rule for all ages and handicaps, in fact for all children, is: No long lectures. Even five minutes is too long if you don't involve the children in the presentation, and the best way to involve the children is to relate the theme to their life experience. If they cannot relate to what you are trying to teach them, they will not understand what is being taught and quickly lose interest. Here is a list of some possible methods of presenting the theme which keep these two cautions in mind.

1. *Storytelling.* Storytelling of Gospel scenes, parables and miracles, as well as storytelling of contemporary real life situations which illustrate your theme, are excellent teaching tools. To be effective you have to relax and be a bit of a ham. Tell the story in your own words. Keep it short and to the point, leaving out complicated and unnecessary details. Ask for the students' comments and opinions as you go along. For example, if you are doing a story about Jesus, relate his feelings and emotions to those of the students. If you say that Jesus was tired and needed a rest so he went out to the countryside, ask whether they ever feel tired and in need of rest and where would they go. Then continue with your story.

Use gesture, voice intonations, pictures or other props that you have available. Exaggerate motions and actions slightly for effect and don't worry if the words come out a little differently in class than when you were practicing at home. You may have to make adjustments as you hear the children's comments and interjections. When you have finished the story, ask for the children's comments. Maybe someone would like to retell it. This could be done especially well in the small groups in which everyone would have a chance to retell it. With older children ask them to retell the story as if it were happening today. Would it come out differently? What would have to be changed? It is interesting to observe what parts of the story different children emphasize. This gives you a clue as to how your students think and what interests them. This is valuable information for a teacher as it helps toward the preparation of future lessons.

2. *Pictures.* Pictures and other visual aides are a must. They are good for illustrating any kind of presentation and for working with a student one to one. The biblical pictures I prefer are those which look like real life presentations from first century Palestine.[2] Others prefer

pictures in the more popular modern art forms. If you have none available and cannot afford to purchase them, your religious education office will probably have some old student manuals or religious magazines out of which you can cut pictures to mount on cardboard. Good nature pictures and family pictures can also be cut out of magazines you might have around the house. As you make your presentation, illustrate it with your pictures, asking the children to comment, to point to the picture and tell you what they see.

    3. *Flannel Board.* A flannel board presentation is another method of storytelling. You can purchase a flannel board or make your own by covering a good size frame (at least 15 × 30) with felt. Flannel board figures come with some lesson plans. They can also be made, or they can be purchased as a complete set for specific stories,[3] such as the feeding of the five thousand, the good Samaritan, and many more. If you are making them, glue a piece of sandpaper to the back of each piece so that your figures will adhere to the felt.

    Never read the story, even though it comes included in the packet with each story. If you try to read it or even to memorize it, you will be too distracted with ''getting it right'' and lose the spontaneity, the effect the story is calculated to achieve. Instead tell the story in your own words, dramatically, inviting the children's comments at calculated moments. In small groups let each child take a turn to tell the story using the flannel board and moving the figures whichever way they prefer. Flannel board stories are a favorite of all special children, and one of the best teaching tools available. With a little practice you will find the flannel board easy and fun to use. If older children seem hesitant to participate, ask them to show the little ones how to do it. They'll soon perceive the challenge and be willing to give it a try.

    4. *Other Audio-Visual Aids.* Slides can be used effectively instead of pictures, but films and filmstrips are usually too lengthy and move too quickly for our students. Keeping eye to eye contact with students is almost always preferable, as in this way you can gauge the timing and effectiveness of your methods.

    5. *Chalkboard.* Although most special children have limited reading ability, a chalkboard is excellent for illustrating your lesson with stick figures or for listing key words and expressions from your lesson. As you write tell the children what you are writing or ask them to tell you what to write. A good icebreaker to get students talking is to ask them to help you make a list of something and write their contributions

on the board. The contents of the list will depend on the theme of the day. For instance, you might ask them to list words that describe what being a Christian means, or words that tell you how you can help other people and make them happy. Children will warm to the task quickly, and soon they will be anxious to get in their opinion and have their contribution written on the board.

6. *Hands on Experience.* Give each child an object, something to make or to look at—maybe a picture, a pretty stone, a lump of clay. Begin a discussion of what they see in front of them. What is it? What can they do with it? What does it mean? What does it look like? Depending on your theme and what you have chosen to give them, lead them through questions, answers and manipulation of the media toward the conclusion you are seeking. For instance:

You have given the students a ball of clay. Ask them to make something God has made. (This is easy, as they can make a moon or sun among other easy things.) Let them tell you what they have chosen to make and what it is good for, why they think God made it, etc. Your immediate objective may be to illustrate the point that all things God made are good and useful. Your long-range objective might be to show that God made them also, and they too are good and useful. This could be followed up by a lesson on the gifts God gives us.

At this point, it might be wise to interject a warning. Not every brilliant idea you have may work, but don't get discouraged. It's better to fail occasionally than to never try anything new, and over the years you will develop a list of successful presentation methods. All the ideas in this book have been tried many times, but we have also had our share of failures, and often it is from these failures that we have gotten some of our best insights.

7. *Role Playing and Drama.* To dramatize or role play your presentation, first tell the story briefly. Then ask the children to role play or dramatize all or part of it. Don't worry about how it will turn out. If you're looking for perfection the children will become inhibited. If you are relaxed the children will be also. If necessary repeat the performance several times so that all children can have a turn.

Give all the children a role and let them speak their part in their own words. If you have children who don't talk, you can read or tell the story as they act. This can be a lot of spontaneous fun, so join in the laughter and be glad if they are learning to laugh at themselves. If, on the other hand, your theme is serious, you will be surprised at how emotional the atmosphere can become and how seriously the children will take their roles. As this type of presentation may take more time, you may want to skip the arts and crafts this week. You may also need to shorten the small groups' time slot for that week, or you may want to make the preparations for the skits in the small groups. Whichever way you choose to do it, it is sure to be memorable.

Scripture

The Scripture reading for the week either is your theme or is used to illustrate your theme. In the first case, your presentation will probably be some form of storytelling followed by an abbreviated reading of the same from the Bible itself. In the second case, your presentation will be followed by a Scripture reading which illustrates your point.

Before class, set up your Scripture center and open the Bible to the day's reading. If possible, chairs are drawn up in a circle. When you are ready to read the Scripture passage, pause for a moment of quiet, light the candle, and proceed as we have detailed earlier in this book in how to use Scripture.

Prayer

Every lesson should flow into and be experienced in prayer. Lessons could begin and end in prayer, but to avoid routinization prayer should also be an integral expression of the lesson itself. Thus the ideal time for prayer is after the presentation and Scripture reading. For details on how to use prayer in your lessons, see Chapter 2 and note the examples at the end of this chapter.

Music

Music is another essential part of your program. Handicapped children, especially the younger ones, love it, and in some cases it quiets and reaches children whom we have found no other way to reach. The child who has never spoken may suddenly try to sing. Children with poor coordination will pick up a rhythm instrument, and music becomes therapy.

Whenever possible, gestures or even dance should accompany the music. March around the room, have a procession at liturgy, dramatize to music or just sit quietly and allow reflective music to prepare the atmosphere for prayer. If the song you are singing has no gestures, make them up. Gestures are an excellent way to teach the words, and for children with speech impairments, gestures and rhythm instruments provide an alternative mode of participation.

Pick easy, catchy tunes with repetitive phrases or choruses in which everyone can chime in. "This Is the Day," "Kumbaya" and "His Banner Over Me Is Love" are old favorites in special religious education centers.[4] Sing the same songs week after week, adding or substituting a new one every now and then. Repetition and "knowing the song" gives children security and a feeling of accomplishment. They will not be bored with the repetition. When picking songs, provide some variety in styles of music and occasionally sing songs that are used at Sunday liturgies.

At your own liturgies, prayer services and sacramental celebrations sing the songs you have been practicing all year. If you are participating in a liturgy with the larger church community and have advance knowledge of what music will be played, help the children become familiar with the music by playing these hymns in class. If you have no recording or guitar player, ask your folk group or choir to make you a tape with which you can practice.

To teach a song, play it first for the children, asking them to listen carefully to the words. Then have them hum it and listen again. Then, taking the song line by line, have them repeat the words. Explain the meaning of the words and show what gestures you will use, if any, to express this meaning. Remember, you will be repeating these songs often, so words and meaning are important and should in some way express the mood and religious conviction of the participants. While it may be difficult to always coordinate the musical theme with the lesson theme, an attempt should be made to at least make a connection. Songs such as those previously mentioned can be related to any number of themes. At the proper moment announce that the lesson is now going to be celebrated in song and explain the connection.

Records such as *Hi God II* by Carey Landry have songs which tell stories covering a wide range of themes. While you may not have time to teach all of these songs, you could use them just to listen to during a prayerful moment. They also make excellent teaching tools for reinforcing your lesson.

Sometimes adolescents, especially boys, go through a stage where they don't like to sing. They will usually, however, be willing to use the rhythm instruments, lead processions and listen quietly to reflective music. The latter, in particular, seems to move them. Remember not to force them to do things which they feel are babyish. Instead find alternative ways for them to participate. As they are often of an age for confirmation, they will probably show some interest in learning the confirmation ceremony songs so that they will be able to participate with confidence on confirmation day.

Having a guitar player or better yet two guitar players to lead the music portion of your program is effective as long as they are also available to play for your liturgies. The advantage of live music is that the tempo and keys can be regulated, thus making it easier to teach a song. Nevertheless, if this is not possible, there are plenty of records and tapes which are easy to sing to and can be transported anywhere.

Arts and Crafts

Before your program begins each year, prepare a large bag or box of supplies which will be either left in the classroom or brought to class each week. You may want one bag for each small group. These bag(s) might include crayons (fat ones for uncoordinated little fingers and thin ones for others), washable magic markers, washable poster paints, brushes, pencils, chalk, scissors, paste, tape, ruler, stars, stapler, clay, paper in different colors and perhaps stencils, tracing paper, a supply of old magazines and religion manuals to cut up, felt, and various other collage materials. Hopefully, you will also either own or have access to some books of religious spirit (duplicating) masters which contain pictures, puzzles, and craft ideas for various lesson themes.[5]

For spur of the moment role playing and dramatics you will not need costumes, but for special occasions you might want to begin collecting some simple props. This would be preferable to asking the parents to provide costumes and then having one child come in an elaborate costume and another in a sheet. Keep costume ideas simple. Perhaps use only hats or signs draped around the neck. Hats for shepherds and disciples can be easily made by draping a pillowcase over the head and forehead and securing it across the forehead and around the back of the head with a rolled scarf or cord. Halos and crowns can be made from cardboard and wire, or redecorate Burger King crowns. Colored and white sheets can be draped and tied to make togas and robes. A baseball hardhat covered with foil and worn backward makes a great Roman soldier helmet. A plume can be added.

Arts and crafts projects should be kept simple and easy to clean up. No matter how simple or sloppy, a project made by the student is always preferable to one that the teacher made. Teachers must perceive the abilities of the students in their small groups and plan the arts and crafts projects accordingly. Projects which students can do with a minimum of assistance and a certain amount of success will give them confidence and spur them on to try harder next time.

The philosophy behind the use of arts and crafts in the classroom is based on the results of the Havinghurst retention tests. These tests show that children remember 10% of what they taste, touch or smell, 20% of what they hear, 30% of what they see or read, 70% of what they say, and *90% of what they do.* We must conclude then that role playing and drama and arts and crafts are primary classroom strategies to increase retention as they represent learning by doing.

Thus, *it is of utmost importance that the arts and crafts part of your program be carefully planned to illustrate and develop the theme of the day.* Coloring just any religious picture is not sufficient. In fact, crayoning can become repetitious and boring if used too often. Poster paint on a large posterboard is both easier and more exciting for the children who are all too often just handed a coloring book and told to sit quietly and color.

As not every teacher is creative artistically, some special effort may be needed to design the arts and crafts part of your program, and for this an arts and crafts director would be valuable. This person could be one of the teachers, or he or she could be solely responsible for helping other teachers prepare this part of their program. Available resources include several good books of arts and crafts ideas,[6] and there are many lesson plans which include these as an integral part. An especially good model for the latter is the set of lesson plans entitled *Teach Me, Please Teach Me.*[7]

While the latter is excellent, it is designed mostly for younger children. For older children and for children with less severe disabilities you may want to adapt some more grown-up ideas from contemporary religious manuals or from publications such as *Celebration.*[8] The following Lenten project was adapted from the latter and completed with much enthusiasm by our older students. Next time we plan to allow the younger ones to contribute, as it is not really difficult, and on seeing the completed project they were very interested in "making one also."

Our oldest students sanded and painted a large (6' × 4') wooden cross for use in Lenten and Easter liturgies, prayer services and dramatic performances. (Use a painter's drop cloth.) As they worked their teacher led a discussion with them on the meaning of the cross, why they were painting it purple, and the fact that Jesus probably assisted his foster father in the carpentry shop as a child.

A lesson was set aside early in Lent to review symbols of our faith. (See caution in Chapter 3.) Stencils were made of these symbols, and each child traced and cut out of colored posterboard one symbol. As part of a prayer service, each child then hammered his or her symbol onto the cross, and, if they wished, said a few words about the symbol they had chosen to make. The cross was later used effectively for both the Lenten penance service and the Easter liturgy.

Putting It All Together

Keeping the above six essential ingredients in mind you can create any number of lessons around a variety of themes. How you will develop a lesson will depend on its place in your lesson sequence for the year. The following is an example.

Each year you have students receiving First Communion and confirmation. You wish then to celebrate a lesson on baptism each year as background for the above sacraments, but as you have many of the same students from year to year you would like to provide some variety and find alternative ways of presenting the topic. Here are two possibilities. Note that each lesson is developed in accord with where it fits in the year's plan and in accord with the principle of the six essential ingredients of every lesson plan.

Baptism in Plan 1. In the fall a lesson on baptism could be part of a sequence of lessons that goes as follows. Week 1—God created the world, and it is good. Week 2—God created me in his image; I am good. Week 3—God made us to live and love together: our families are our first community. Week 4—We belong to many communities and one of these is the Church. *Week 5—We join the Church community through baptism.* Week 6—Baptism, Communion, confirmation (sacraments of initiation). Week 7—Thanking God for his creation and each other (our communities). Week 8—Thanksgiving liturgy. (Such a sequence would have to be adjusted to fit your calendar as indicated in the previous chapter and in Appendix I, Plan 4.)

In week 4 you have had a discussion centering on what joining something means and concluded with the concept that joining the Church means becoming a Christian. You have mentioned that you join the Church through baptism and suggested that the students ask their parents to tell them of their (the students') baptism.

Now (week 5) you want to make the point that baptism is an important moment in our lives because it is a sign that God is calling us, inviting us to embrace each other in community with the same love with which he embraces us. You might develop the lesson as follows.

You arrive early, put music on, and post pictures of baptisms in key locations. The children arrive, and as an early bird special you give them a follow-the-dots picture of a baptism to complete and color. Your presentation begins with a brief review of last week's lesson and invitation to share anything they may have learned from their parents of their own baptism. Then you restate the concept that through baptism we join the Church and become Christians, and you conclude with the question: "What does being Christian mean?" Continue by compiling on the board a list of words which might describe a Christian. Each word suggested by the children is posted, then discussed by all and commented on by you. Conclusion—baptism is an important event in our lives as it requires us to love one another and show it by our actions and words.

This is followed by the Scripture reading (Jn 3:1–8) and spontaneous prayer asking God to help us live up to our baptismal commitment. The song "His Banner Over Me Is Love" (*Hi God I*) or "Children of the Lord" (*Hi God II*) concludes the first half hour of your classtime.

In the small groups using the baptismal pictures, teachers discuss the actual ceremony, concentrating on the baptism itself. Children finish the pictures begun earlier and discuss content with aides. A role play of a baptism concludes the lesson.

Baptism in Plan 2. An alternative time to discuss baptism would be in the context of Jesus' life and ministry. This might be done the first week after the Christmas and New Year holidays, and be part of a two week sequence as follows: Week 1—Jesus' baptism; the beginning of his ministry. Week 2—Like Jesus we also are baptized and have a ministry.

Week 1: As an early bird special you could have the children draw a picture telling something about their Christmas or have them make a circle and take turns telling each other about their Christmas. The presentation could be a flannel board storytelling of Jesus' baptism or a simple storytelling with pictures pointing out that his baptism was the beginning of Jesus' ministry. Student-teacher dialogue could concentrate on the fact that we also have been baptized as Jesus was, and that as Jesus was called by the Father, so are we. A candle could then be lit and Matthew 3:13–17 read, followed by a prayer thanking God for sending us Jesus and asking him to help us to grow to be like Jesus. "Kumbaya" ("Someone's Praying, Lord, Be With Us") would be an appropriate song, beginning with the line "Someone's thanking, Lord, be with us." This can be sung a cappella very effectively.

Small groups could make a collage of baptismal pictures around a picture of Jesus' baptism or surround a picture of Jesus' baptism with pictures of themselves and a quotation such as "Follow me" (Jn 21:19). (If you are not going to take the pictures yourself, be sure you call the parents to send them in.) As the collage or poster is being made children should be encouraged to discuss the pictures and review the presentation. Homework could be to ask their parents to tell them about their baptism. (I do not usually recommend homework, as the message rarely gets home, and the idea is a bit too academic. Nevertheless, an occasional request such as the above could be considered, provided parents are informed separately.)

Week 2: Presentation time could be taken up by sharing the stories of our baptisms and by role playing a baptism. Scripture could be John 3:1–8, which, combined with a singing of "Kumbaya" and a renewal of the baptismal promises, is all you need for an effective prayer service. Small groups could discuss what being a Christian means. To illustrate the answer, a game which necessitates cooperation, sharing, or helping one another could be played.[9]

These then are just a few ideas on how a specific lesson idea could be developed. Hopefully, these samples will inspire you to develop your own lesson plans, remembering that in addition to the six essential ingredients, a logical sequence (from lesson to lesson), review, repetition and simplicity (one theme at a time) must be taken into consideration. Depending on the age and learning level of the students, the small groups can display more individuality in developing the lesson themes.

If you need further inspiration, there are listed in the bibliography several good books of lesson plans from which you can adapt lesson plans and arts and crafts projects to fit your plans. Look also at lesson plans from major publishers designed for children of the same age as your students and see if there are any ideas in them that you can use. We have used the format of Sadlier's confirmation journal with children with simple learning disabilities and found it a good project for the confirmation year. The journal can be put together and xeroxed in an order that coordinates its progression with your overall year's plan.

Notes

1. Donald Rogers, *In Praise of Learning,* Abingdon, Nashville, 1980. Rogers tells us that his research indicates that the teachers from whom students learned most were those noted for their dependability— those who were always there.

2. Pictures available from David C. Cook Publishing Co., Elgin, Ill., and Providence Lithograph Co. (*Bible Teaching Pictures,* 1962).

3. Flannel board sets are available from David C. Cook Publishers, Elgin, Ill., and Standard Publishing Co., Cincinnati, Ohio.

4. Songs from *Hi God I* and *Hi God II* by Carey Landry, North American Liturgy Resources, Phoenix, Arizona, 1975.

5. Spirit masters available from a variety of sources. Most recently we have used those from *Arena Lettres,* 8 Lincoln, Waldwick, N.J. 07463 and Ikonographics, P.O. Box 4454, Louisville, Ky. 40204.

6. For books of arts and crafts ideas see bibliography.

7. Dahl, *op. cit.*

8. *Celebration,* National Catholic Reporter, Kansas City, Mo. 64141.

9. Dahl, *op. cit.*

8

Preparing a Liturgy

I have hesitated to prepare a separate chapter on preparing liturgies, as the topic has been alluded to in so many other places. However, as I know that having all the information together in one place is useful, I shall just list a few ideas here with the understanding that reading Chapter 2, which includes sacramental celebrations, is a necessary complement to this chapter.

Worship, as already stated, must be integral to any program you put together, as it is one of the primary ways we meet the risen Christ and open ourselves to the Spirit. Liturgies and prayer moments (sometimes called paraliturgies), prepared for the whole community (that includes parents, siblings and friends as well as students, teachers and aides) are also ways of celebrating our Christian unity and commitment to one another. These moments are meant to be joyful, faith-filled experiences in which the children can participate comfortably. In some sense then the worship experience must belong to them, and the best way to achieve this is by allowing them to help in both the preparation and the production.

At least three weeks before the liturgy the teachers should consult with each other. The theme of the liturgy has already been noted on the year's plan (see Chapter 6), and is continuous with present class time themes. Readings and celebrating materials are now chosen to reinforce this continuity. Students will be needed to serve at the altar, prepare prayers, read, bring up the gifts, distribute programs and make decorations. Short of creating mass confusion the more students involved the better.

Teachers then consult with their groups. Some students may wish to prepare something to bring to the altar during the offertory procession. This could include birthday cards for Jesus, New Year or Lenten promises, confirmation journals, food for the needy, flowers, prayer requests, or anything they have made in class that pertains to the theme.

Others may wish to prepare posters, banners or garlands, etc. Still others might prepare a short skit or role play illustrating the Gospel message for the day.

Volunteers are asked to do the readings. These readings may be abbreviated or not according to the ability of the student.[1] Type them up, double spaced, and make sure they get home a week in advance as parents will want to practice with their children. Type up a program for the day of the liturgy which includes the readings so that parents and friends can follow what is being read. Drop one of these programs off at the rectory to remind the celebrant of the theme to which the homily will be directed. That the celebrant will be available that day has already been ascertained when making the year's plan, but if for any reason you have failed to do this, or the priest or minister is suddenly unavailable, proceed with a prayer service instead. These community moments are too important to do without.

Every liturgy should include music with which the children are familiar, a chance to move around a bit and silent time. Rhythm instruments are joyous, but should be collected immediately after their use. It is easiest to use them for the entrance hymn and then collect them. Joyous and more noisy moments should be balanced by quiet meditative ones during which you play reflective music or sing a hymn with a quieting, reverent effect, such as "Kumbaya" or "Hear, O Lord, the Sound of My Call." An offertory procession and/or gathering of the students around the altar for the Liturgy of the Eucharist is a good change of pace and encourages attentive participation.

Otherwise children should be seated as a group in the front rows with aides at strategic places. Keeping the students together makes it easier for the priest or minister to dialogue with them during the homily. If very hyperactive children are present, assign aides to them individually and seat them at the ends of rows so that if they are too restless an easy exit can be maneuvered. While an attentive attitude is desirable, try not to squelch all spontaneity by insisting that children do not move or speak unless asked to do so. They have already had enough of this in their lives. Hyperactive children occasionally escaping their aides are not a disaster, but rather an opportunity to affirm our commitment to their being-with-us. Your celebrant will probably be able to accommodate to this.

You might also consider having a more informal liturgy in a teachers' lounge or sitting room where students sit on the floor in a semi-circle around the celebrant. This intimate atmosphere is conducive to spontaneous shared prayer.

Liturgies are, of course, appropriate in any season, but those events we celebrate most frequently in our liturgical year are "Back Together Again"[2] (in September), Creation or St. Francis Day (October), Thanksgiving, Advent, Christmas, Baptism, Jesus Shows Us the Way, Jesus Heals Us, Lent, Easter, Jesus Feeds Us, First Communion, Confirmation, Coming of the Spirit, Hand in Hand, Celebrate Summer (good for a picnic). Possible ways to celebrate these different events are scattered throughout this book. Here are a few additional ideas. Perhaps they will inspire you to do something even better.

For Advent and Christmas liturgies we have used some of the following ideas, varying them a little from year to year.

1. While the priest, minister or other adult leader reads the good news (a combination of Matthew and Luke so that one can have shepherds and wise men), children dramatize the reading in front of the altar. If your group is large, little ones could form an angel choir. Different parts of the story are interspersed with appropriate carols such as "Silent Night," "We Three Kings," and "O Come, All Ye Faithful." This scenario replaces the reading of the Gospel and the homily.

2. A large crèche with figures has been borrowed for the liturgy. The empty stable is in place in front of the altar. As the Gospel is read, children place the figures in the stable. If you have more students than figures, add straw, stars, angels, greenery, flowers or gifts.

3. On either side of the altar or stable place a small bare Christmas tree. At the offertory students hang on the branches decorated cardboard or styrofoam ornaments on which they have written their names or put a picture of themselves plus something they would like to give Jesus for Christmas. If you are having a prayer service instead of a liturgy, you might want to combine suggestions 2 and 3.

4. For an Advent Liturgy a lighting of the candles on the Advent wreath is effective. Lighted candles are always a fascination. Four students light the candles while four more read the prayers they have prepared to go with the lighting. The theme could be "Prepare Ye the Way of the Lord," and the song by the same name from Godspell could accompany a processional in liturgical dance form. (Use very simple gestures.) A gradual lighting of the room or chapel is also effective, especially if the liturgy is celebrated after twilight.

5. Advent and Christmas themes could be combined in a prayer service which moves from the Advent candle lighting to the stable.

6. Easter or Lenten liturgies could include a procession with palms or a tableau of the Last Supper including the foot-washing. A prayer service might feature a seder. If your students have made a cross as described in the previous chapter, this cross could now be used for a re-enactment of the Way of the Cross with students taking the parts of Simon, Veronica, Jesus, the women, the disciples and the crowd. Again, this playlet would take the place of the Gospel and homily or be the centerpiece of a prayer service.

7. A Creation or St. Francis' Day liturgy could be celebrated by the students bringing in their favorite stuffed animals to place around the altar as they sing, "He's Got the Whole World in His Hands." Such a liturgy could also substitute a rendition of St. Francis' *Canticle to the Sun* or his *Peace Prayer* for the first reading or the Communion meditation.

On Valentine's Day or Mother's Day children could make something to present to their parents at the liturgy. Father's Day would be a good time for an outdoor liturgy and picnic.

Consider some innovations. Clowns, puppets, and mime or liturgical dance can present Gospel themes to special persons in ways that words can often not accomplish. If you have these kind of resources in your communities, avail yourself of them. These artists are usually very dedicated and often willing to donate their time.

How many times a year you celebrate liturgy will depend on your situation, but as mentioned in Chapter 2, once a month is not too often. When liturgy is an expression of your community's religious sentiment, there is no better way of evoking Christian conversion and commitment. Thus it is important that you use the ideas above, those from the liturgy appendix and those from the children's liturgy books listed in the bibliography only to stimulate your own creativity, your own ideas. The best liturgies are always those that are prepared and celebrated together as community gift to the Father and to each other.

Notes

1. For comments about abridging readings see Chapter 2.

2. "Back Together Again" is a song on Sadlier's First Grade record, 1974.

Conclusion

As Thomas Aquinas lay dying, he had a religious experience which led him to remark that all his work, his comprehensive *Summa,* his many writings, seemed like so many straws compared to that which had been revealed to him.

On completing this book and rereading what I have written over the last year and a half, I have a little bit of the same feeling. Working with the handicapped is a kind of religious experience, and the straws that we offer do seem a bit pale in comparison to the gifts our students bring us. As Jean Vanier once said, ''If one listens to the weak, they will guide us to the truth.''[1]

Nevertheless, like all of us the handicapped need to know they are lovable and capable, to recognize their God-given potential and the love of God within them. This they can only discover through others.

Our task as teachers, then, is to explore ways to reach out to our handicapped brothers and sisters, to all special persons, and to offer them loving companionship on their journey. It is my hope that all those who have picked up and read all or part of this book have found something in it which will help them in their particular ministry and inspire them to yet greater works in Jesus' name.

And the disciples were troubled for it seemed that Jesus was abandoning them. But he understood their fears and assured them, ''The man who has faith in me will do the works I do, and greater far than these'' (Jn 14:12).

Note

1. *National Catholic Reporter,* September 2, 1983, p. 7.

Part Three

Appendices

Annotated Bibliography and Resource Guide for Special Religious Education

The contents of this bibliography is limited to books which are still in print or readily available and to books with which the author is familiar and has found useful. Limitations of various resources are noted in the appended comments.

Background Material

In order to integrate the handicapped into the life of the Church community, some background material is indispensable.

Bissonnier, Henri, *The Pedagogy of Resurrection*. N.Y., Paulist Press, 1979. The best there is! This 225-page book deals with the handicapped. Both philosophical and practical, this book is a must for anyone working in special religious education.

Bogardus, LaDonna, *Christian Education for Retarded Persons*. Nashville, Abingdon Press, 1971. A good manual for interdenominational programs. A little out of date, but still better than some more recent publications. May be found in most libraries.

Elkind, David, *Children and Adolescents, Interpretive Essays on Jean Piaget*. N.Y., Oxford University Press, 1981. Piaget's studies on how children think and learn have important educational implications which are well pointed out in this book. While this book does not look directly at developmentally impaired children, the implications will be obvious to anyone working in special religious education. Highly recommended.

Hahn, Hans R. and Werner H. Raasch, *Helping the Retarded To Know God. A Guide for Christian Teachers of the Mentally Handicapped.* St. Louis, Concordia Publishing House, 1969. Good for the training of teachers of an interdenominational group. Valuable background information for understanding the handicapped. Also a bit out of date.

Hogan, Griff, editor. *The Church and Disabled Persons.* Springfield, Ill.: Templegate Publishers, 1983. What rights have disabled persons as Christians and as citizens? What responsibilities toward the disabled have the churches and the government? Essays by Jean Vanier and others knowledgeable in the field. This would be a good book for parents and those working with special adults.

U.S. Catholic Conference, *Pastoral Statement of U.S. Catholic Bishops on Handicapped People,* November 16, 1978. Important for Catholics.

Vanier, Jean, *Eruption to Hope.* N.Y., Paulist Press, 1971. Still the classic and best plea for the poor, lonely, forgotten handicapped of the world. Something by Vanier is a must for those working with the handicapped. His more recent titles, also available from Paulist Press, include *Community and Growth* (1980) and *The Challenge of L'Arche* (1981).

How-To Manuals for Teachers of Special Religious Education

Britschgi, B. and K. Jennings, *Special Religious Education: Catechist Formation and Resource Book.* San Diego, Diocese of San Diego, 1981. A 50 page pamphlet. Good insights and suggestions. Bibliography out of date as most recommended books are out of print and hard to locate.

Haskett, Sr. M. Sheila, O.S.F. *Journey with Jesus: Director's Hand-*

book. Milwaukee, Cardinal Stritch College Bookstore, 1977. To be used with *Journey with Jesus* curriculum series.

O'Donnell, Brigid, *We Care: A Guidebook for Special Education Catechists,* Catholic Education Center, Archdiocese of St. Paul/ Minneapolis, revised 1983. Concise 50 page pamphlet with insightful and compassionate tips for the beginning catechist in special religious education.

O'Donnell, Brigid, *Religious Education and the Learning Disabled Child.* Catholic Education Center, Archdiocese of St. Paul/ Minneapolis. A 10 page pamphlet with some valuable hints. About the only thing around on the subject. Good for a start.

Wood, Andrew, *Unto the Least of These.* Shepherds Inc., The regular Baptist Agency for the Mentally Retarded, Union Grove, Wis. A sound and comprehensive 40 page guidebook for setting up a Sunday school for special children.

Books of Lesson Plans

Black, Sister Mary Maurice, S.S.J., *Jesus Our Best Friend, His Ancestry and Life.* Watertown, N.Y., 1982. 76 pp. $4.10. Good ideas for crafts and music accompany these lesson plans.

Celebration, National Catholic Reporter, Kansas City, Mo. A monthly guide for liturgy preparation for adults, children and for in the home. Ideas are adaptable for classroom instruction if you are following the liturgical year. Very valuable resource.

Clark, Dorothy, *et al., Teach Me, Please Teach Me.* Elgin, Ill., David C. Cook, 1974. 12 of the best lesson plans around. Intended for younger children, but some can be adapted for youth. Follow-up ideas can expand material another 20 weeks. Many themes similar to those in appendix of year and lesson plans. Highly recommended.

Haskett, Sister M. Sheila, O.S.F., *Journey with Jesus.* Cardinal Stritch College, Milwaukee, Wis., 1978. Largest series available.

Sacramentally and theologically oriented. Comes as three sets: *Call to Communion, Call to Reconciliation* and *Call to Confirmation*. Each set covers three years with 20 lessons for each year.

Haskett, Sister M. Sheila, O.S.F., *Journey With Jesus—Gospel Study,* Cardinal Stritch College, Milwaukee, Wis., 1978. Covers three year cycle. Sets of illustrations for each Sunday are excellent and can be purchased separately and copied for your students.

Keith-Lucas, Alan, *Christian Education for Emotionally Disturbed Children.* National Council of Churches, N.Y., revised ed. An excellent resource for those working with emotionally disturbed children in residential centers or in community settings for emotionally disturbed only.

O'Donnell, Brigid M., *Adapting the Joy Series for Persons with Mental Retardation,* Winston Press, 1978.

Podlasek, Sister Carol, *Gift.* Winston Press, 1976. A two year Communion preparation program. Still one of the best things around, especially for young children. Accompanying set of pictures to make your own flannel board stories.

Uhl, Catherine Geary, *Gospel Lesson Plans.* Paulist Press, 1979.

Weber, Sister Bernadette, O.S.B., units on natural symbols: *Water, Rock, Seeds, Fire and Light.* Also lesson plans based on the Sunday Gospels. Current cycle available. Bureau of Education, Diocese of St. Cloud, Minn. $3 per set. Very good!

Consider also adapting lessons for little ones from Sadlier, Silver Burdett, Benziger, and Christ Our Life Series.

Newsletters and Resource Catalogues

Black, Sister Mary Maurice, *Teach Them As Jesus Did.* Catechetical Office, Watertown, N.Y., 1980. This handbook for special religious educators contains the most complete resource guide available anywhere for special religious education. It includes where to purchase your audio-visual materials and a comprehensive list of what is available: also an annotated bibliography. Many of the books in the latter are out of print, but Sister indicates where in New York State they are available.

National Apostolate with Mentally Retarded Persons Resource Guide, Publication Office, Jefferson, Wis. Valuable and up to date annotated bibliography.

NAMRP (National Apostolate with Mentally Retarded Persons) Newsletter and Journal. Newsletter published six times a year; Journal published quarterly. Publication Office, Jefferson, Wis. Excellent.

SPRED Newsletter, Published monthly September through May. Order from SPRED Publications, 1025 W. Fry St. Chicago, Ill. 60622.

Liturgy Resources

Directory for Masses with Children, Pub. V291, $1.25 and *Eucharistic Prayers for Children,* Pub. V387B $3.25; order both from USCCB—Office of Religious Studies, 1312 Mass. Ave. N.W., Washington, D.C. 20005. If you are Catholic, these are important to have, especially the latter.

Gamm, Rev. David, *On Cloud Nine.* Notre Dame, Ind.: Ave Maria Press, 1976.

Jamison, Andrew, *Liturgies for Children.* Cincinnati, Ohio: St. Anthony Messenger Press, 1980. Good adaptable ideas.

Celebration, National Catholic Reporter, Kansas City, Mo. 64141. The best though not intended specifically for special persons. A monthly publication with liturgy ideas for each Sunday for adults and children. Excellent.

Kenny, Bernadette, R.S.H.M., *Children's Liturgies,* N.Y.: Paulist Press, 1977. Many of these ideas could be adapted for special children.

McIntyre, Marie, *Religion Teacher's Pet.* Mystic, Conn.: Twenty-Third Pub. Good ideas.

New Life Liturgies 1-3. N.Y.: Sadlier. Very simple, but effective ideas for little ones. A good place to begin.

Rezy, Carol, *Liturgies for Little Ones,* Notre Dame, Ind.: Ave Maria Press, 1978. Good adaptable ideas. My favorite.

Music

Records and tapes and often sheet music available.

Landry, Rev. Carey, *Hi God I,* North American Liturgy Resources, Phoenix, Arizona 1973. Contains such favorites as "His Banner Over Me Is Love" and "Joy, Joy, Joy." Landry's songs are excellent as many of them have much repetition and are easy for special children to learn. Often record has children singing; thus key is also just right.

Landry, Rev. Carey, *Hi God II,* North American Liturgy Resources, Phoenix, Arizona, 1973. This record is even better as songs chronicle the important steps in the life of Jesus. Many are good just to listen to during a prayer moment. Others great for singing and dancing. Favorites include "If I Were a Butterfly" (for little ones) and for all "This is the Day," "Peace Is Flowing Like a River," and "We Come To Your Table."

Sadlier's First Grade Record and some others have good, repetitious or easy to learn songs. Favorites are "Hurray for God" and "Sometimes It's Not Easy."

Wise, Joe, *Gonna Sing My Lord.* Cincinnati, Ohio: World Library of Sacred Music, 1966. Contains good songs for liturgy, "Take Our Bread" and others.

Audio-Visuals

This is a limited list. It contains only the most basic and essential materials and not all of these. For a complete listing see *Teach Them as Jesus Did* by Sister Maurice Black, listed under Newsletters and Resource Catalogs in the bibliography.

Spirit Masters, sometimes known as duplicating masters or ditto masters, are books of pictures to color and creative learning activities that you can reproduce on a duplicating machine and use in religious education classrooms. They come prepared for different age levels and are topic oriented: Life of Jesus, Eucharist, Church, etc. Send to companies for complete lists of available materials. Most books intended for children over 9 years of age are too difficult for special children. We have used the two sources below:

Arena Lettres, 8 Lincoln Pl., Waldwick, N.J. 07463.
Ikonographics, Inc., *Work and Pray Series,* P.O. Box 4454, Louisville, Ky. 40204. The Apple Activity Series are good for little ones. They have filmstrips to go with each ditto book. (This is something new we haven't tried yet.)

Flannel Board Sets are a must for people working with special children as the children after a demonstration can do these themselves. Two sources we have used are:

David C. Cook Publishing Co., Elgin, Ill. (Ask for list of stories available.)
Standard Publishing Co., Cincinnati, Ohio.

Bible Pictures are available from:
David C. Cook Publishing Co., Elgin, Ill.
Providence Lithograph Co.

Arts and Crafts Ideas

Pack-O-Fun, Park Ridge, Ill.: Clapper Publishing Co. Inc. This is an arts and crafts magazine published monthly. Good ideas for our programs.

Hagans, Marilyn, *All Good Gifts: Crafts for Christian Gift-Giving.* Ramsey, N.J.: Paulist Press, 1983.

Straatveit, Tytne, *et al. Easy Art Lessons, K-6,* Parker Pub. Co. West Nyack, N.Y., 1979.

Audio-Visuals About the Handicapped

Blessed Be: An eight minute movie by Paulist Productions with words taken directly from the Sermon on the Mount. The mentally handicapped dramatize each beautitude. Beautiful.

The Heart Has Its Reasons: A videotape available from Journey Communications, Mt. Vernon, Va. A one hour videotape about Jean Vanier and L'Arche, the community for mentally handicapped men and women that he began in 1964 in Trosly-Breuil, a village on the edge of the Compiegne forest about an hour north of Paris. Outstanding!

The Kids on the Block: A live puppet show about children with handicaps who might live on your block. Wonderful for all ages, especially elementary. Not intended for the handicapped children themselves. For information contact Thompson Park Services, Lincroft, N.J.

Retreats

HEC stands for Handicapped Encounter Christ. HEC weekend retreats for the handicapped were started in 1973 by John Keck. These retreats are now given all over the country. Physically disabled are welcome. It was begun for adults, but teenagers are welcome. For information write John Keck, 35 Creighton Lane, Briarcliff Manor, N.Y. 10510 or call 914-941-8688.

Appendix I

An Appendix of Year Plans with Lesson Suggestions

The following are four possible year plans prepared according to the guidelines in Chapters 6 and 7. The first three plans incorporate, whenever appropriate, a reading or psalm response from the lectionary for the Sunday liturgy following your weekly lesson. The lectionary is used primarily by Catholics, Anglicans, Lutherans and Methodists and follows a three year liturgical cycle. A lectionary (or Sunday Missal) can be purchased at most religious bookstores.

The fourth plan is similar in content to the other three, but contains no intentional correspondence to the Sunday readings. If you wish to use plans 1-3, but do not use a lectionary, simply call the first one "week 1" and proceed. The 25th Sunday of Ordinary Time is usually in the middle of September.

All lessons can be developed in a variety of ways. Details are left deliberately vague at times, as we encourage expanding them in accordance with your particular needs. Assistant teachers should develop the weekly themes in their small groups in a manner appropriate for their groups' age/learning level.

SIOT = Sunday in Ordinary Time
SOE = Sunday of Easter

Plan 1—Using Cycle A to B

25th SIOT—Opening Liturgy. Theme: *Back Together Again.* Use song by that name from Sadlier 1 (1974) and include psalm response for that week: "The Lord is near to all who call upon him" (Ps 45).

26th SIOT—If you have not opened last week, use above. Otherwise, Theme: *Called Together To Try and Say Yes to God's Will.*

93

Use Gospel for week (Mt 21:28–32). Sing "Hurray for God" (Sadlier, 1974).

27th SIOT—Theme: *God Made the World and It Is Good.* Gospel: Genesis 1 (use key sentences that are easily understood). Theme could be developed along ecological, stewardship of earth, lines (it is our responsibility not to throw garbage around, pollute, etc.). Use "Hurray for God" again and maybe "He's Got the Whole World in His Hands."

28th SIOT—Theme: *God Made Me and I Am Good.* Use Psalm 23 from 28th SIOT. Continue songs from previous weeks. Perhaps make poster with everyone's picture on it; under each you write different gifts or talents of each student.

29th SIOT—Theme: *God Gave Us Each Other To Live in Loving Community.* Some discussion of the purpose of Church, families, religion class and other communities to which we belong. Use Gospel for week—Mt 22:15–21 (Caesar's coin). Gospel reminds us that we are called to turn to God first, and supportive communities help us do this. This could also be a more simple lesson on what is the Church. Same songs, but add "We Come to Your Table" (*Hi God II*). This lesson could be done as a liturgy.

30th SIOT—Theme: *Love God and Love Neighbor* from Gospel for 30th SIOT (Mt 22:34–40). In prayer moments use response for week, "I love you, Lord, my strength" (Ps 18). Sing same songs. Make signs for rooms at home, "Love God—Love Neighbor."

31st SIOT—Theme: *How Do I Love My Neighbor?* Use beatitudes and responsorial psalm for 31st SIOT, "In you, Lord, have I found my peace" (Ps 131). Start singing "His Banner Over Me Is Love" (*Hi God I*). Could begin making banner, last week or this, for Thanksgiving liturgy, saying "Love God and Neighbor."

32nd SIOT—Theme: Either continue last week's theme or do a lesson on prayer as the way to love God. Continue same songs and art project for Thanksgiving liturgy.

33rd SIOT—Theme: *Using Your Gifts To Love God and Neighbor.* This ties it all together in preparation for next week's celebration at which you might want to bring canned goods to share with those in need. Use Gospel for 33rd SIOT (Mt 25:14–30) on talents. Decide who will read what next week and send home copies to practice.

Feast of Christ the King—Thanksgiving liturgy and social afterward. Have all work of students displayed either at liturgy or social.

Begin Cycle B

Advent 1—Often no class as it is Thanksgiving week. Otherwise do meaning of Advent—*Jesus Is Our Light*. Make a candle or Advent wreath or Advent calendar. Start singing songs you plan to use for Christmas or Advent celebration.

Advent 2—Theme: *Prepare Ye the Way of the Lord*. One could play song by that name in prayer moment, but it is hard to sing. Use Gospel for Advent 2 (Mk 1:1–8) and discuss role of John the Baptist. Perhaps explain about waiting—John waited, Mary waited, we all sometimes wait for special events. Sing Christmas songs and plan celebration.

Advent 3 & 4: Use these weeks to plan and practice Christmas liturgy and party. Perhaps plan a dramatization of birth of Jesus combining Matthew and Luke so that you can have shepherds and astrologers. If you are not having class on Advent 4 you may have to reschedule this for Advent 2 and 3.

Epiphany (January 6 or Sunday between January 2–8)—Theme: *Bringing Our Gifts to Jesus*. Gospel: Mt 2:1–12. Take time to talk with children about their Christmas and New Year celebrations. Think and pray together how in the New Year we will bring ourselves as gifts to Jesus in new ways. This might include helping others who need us, etc. Sing "This Is the Day" (*Hi God II*).

Baptism of the Lord—This week is omitted some years, so check carefully when preparing your calendar. If not—Theme: *Baptism*. Develop lesson plan as in Chapter 7. Sing "This Is the Day" and some other songs you have been practicing.

2nd SIOT—Theme: *Here I Am, Lord*. Use 1st reading for 2nd Sunday (1 Sam 3:3–10, 19). Play song by same name for prayer meditation. Talk of how we are all called as were the first disciples. Discuss baptism and confirmation as ways of celebrating our being called.

3rd SIOT—Theme: *Teach Me Your Ways, O Lord.* Use this psalm (Ps 25) for 3rd SIOT and reading of Mk 1:14–20 (call of the fishermen). Continue previous week's discussion emphasizing confirmation as saying yes to Jesus' call. Plan a confirmation investiture service for next week. This could be a liturgy with social afterward. Sing confirmation songs.

4th SIOT—Theme: *Confirmation Investiture Liturgy.* Present each youth preparing for confirmation with a small gift. Use psalm response for 4th SIOT, "If today you hear his voice, harden not your hearts" (Ps 95). Use confirmation songs such as "Here I Am, Lord," "Peace Is Flowing Like a River" (*Hi God II*) and "The Spirit Is Moving" (Sadlier).

5th SIOT—Theme: *Jesus Feeds Us.* Use Scripture of feeding of the five thousand; it can be done on flannel board or role play. Briefly link it to the Last Supper and today's Eucharistic Liturgy. You will later pick up on this theme again. Sing "We Come To Your Table" (*Hi God II*), "His Banner Over Me Is Love" (*Hi God I*), and/or continue with confirmation songs.

6th SIOT—Theme: *Jesus Heals.* Use Gospel for 6th SIOT about healing of leper (Mk 1:40–45). Discuss what healing means. Physical healing happened occasionally in Jesus' and his disciples' time as it does today, but it is to be understood as a sign of the power of Jesus to heal the spirit—to address the evil in the world through his healing spirit. For prayer meditation use a healing song from *Hi God II.*

7th SIOT—Theme: *Jesus Forgives.* Use Gospel for 7th SIOT about healing of paralytic (Mk 2:1–12). Sing "Peace Is Flowing Like a River" (*Hi God II*).

8th SIOT—Theme *The Ten Commandments.* Use story of ten commandments.

9th SIOT—Theme: *The Law and The Spirit.* Use Gospel for 9th SIOT about picking grain on the sabbath (Mk 2:23–28). Make a big LOVE sign and show how this is the spirit of the law (the ten commandments). Sing "His Banner Over Me Is Love" (*Hi God I*) and/or "Peace Is Flowing Like a River" (*Hi God II*).

Lent 1—Theme: *Thinking About Our Sins.* Use Gospel for Lent 1 (Mk 1:12–15). Use guided prayer exercise in Chapter 2.

Lent 2—Theme: *Reconciliation.* Jesus calls us all to reconciliation with God as we also must be reconciled to each other in his name.

Review call of disciples, Matthew the tax collector, Simon the Zealot, Mary Magdalene, eating with Pharisees, etc. Use "Here I Am, Lord" for prayer meditation. Sing "Peace Is Flowing Like a River" (*Hi God II*).

Lent 3—Theme: *Communal Penance Service*. See Appendix II. Perhaps omit social afterward as a sign of giving up something.

Lent 4—Theme: *The Last Supper*. Tell story linking it to Eucharistic Liturgy. Do role play, letting children take turns being Jesus and later the priest.

Lent 5—Preparation for Palm Sunday and Holy Week. Perhaps plan a walking of the Way of the Cross.

Week before Palm Sunday—Have an Easter liturgy or the Stations, prayer moment or Last Supper role play. For social serve different kinds of bread and grape juice. Sing "This Is the Day" and "Allelu" (Ray Repp).

2nd SOE—Theme: *The Resurrection*. Use Gospel for 2nd SIOT (Jn 20:19–31). Tell stories of Jesus' appearances and explain meaning of this to us. Doubting Thomas theme and forgiveness of sins are alternate possibilities for this Gospel which is used each year for 2nd SIOT.

3rd SOE—Theme: *The Risen Christ*. Use Gospel for this week (Lk 24:35–48). Consider another account of the appearance of Jesus to the disciples behind locked doors and perhaps the Emmaus story. Link Scripture to children's lives pointing out that this is what Jesus was doing at Emmaus and in this passage. Continue "Allelu" (Ray Repp), "This Is the Day" and/or songs you plan for confirmation or Communion liturgy.

4th SOE—Theme: *Good Shepherd*. John 10:11–18 is Gospel for this week. Consider using this week and next to discuss our relationship to the risen Christ, the Church and the community in the Holy Spirit.

5th SOE—Theme: *The Vine and the Branches*. John 15:1–8 continues last week's theme. This would make a good art project. Have a guided prayer meditation in which children are asked to imagine themselves holding hands with Jesus who passes his strength to us all through the linked hands.

6th SOE—This would be a good week for a liturgy: First Communion, final celebration, or confirmation. Readings deal with Jesus' commission to love one another (Jn 15) and Peter's meeting with Cornelius (Acts 10:25–48) during which Peter is convinced that Jesus came for all people.

Most programs would have concluded for the summer by now, but if not, here are the pertinent readings for the weeks until Pentecost around which lessons could be built.
Ascension—Mk 16:15–20
7th SOE—Jn 17:11–18
Pentecost—Acts 2:1–11

Plan 2—Using Cycle B to C

25th SIOT—Opening Liturgy. Theme: *Back Together Again* or *One in the Spirit*. Sing simple repetitious songs such as "This Is the Day" (*Hi God II*) or "Kumbaya" ("'Someone's Loving God, Be with Us'"). Social afterward with perhaps a brief parents' meeting to pass out schedules, etc.

26th SIOT—Opening Liturgy as above or use theme of tolerance from this week's readings: *All People Are Called*. Sing "His Banner Over Me Is Love" (*Hi God I*).

27th SIOT—Theme: *God Made Man and Woman*. Use 1st reading for 27th SIOT (Gen 2:18–24). God made us and we are good. God made man and woman of one flesh to be equal and coworkers for the Lord.

28th SIOT—Theme: *God Made the World and We Are Its Stewards*. Use key concepts from Genesis 1. Sing "He's Got the Whole World in His Hands" and "His Banner Over Me Is Love" (*Hi God I*). Stress what students can do to care for world.

29th SIOT—Theme: *God Made Us To Serve One Another*. Use Gospel of 29th SIOT (Mk 10:42–45). Continue songs from last week. Have practical demonstration of serving one another.

30th SIOT—Theme: *When We Serve One Another We See Jesus* (As Did *Bartimaeus*). Use Mark 10:45–52 to illustrate that the purpose of our weekly meetings is to learn to see and know Jesus so that we can better serve one another.

31st SIOT—Theme: *Love God and Love Neighbor*. Use Gospel for 31st SIOT (Mk 12:28–34) to illustrate the message Jesus brings us about what God wants of us. Sing "His Banner Over Me Is Love" (*Hi God I*).

32nd SIOT—Theme: *How Do We Love Our Neighbor?* Let students tell you and then, using Gospel for week (Mk 12:41–44), show how giving of self is key.

33rd SIOT—Theme: *How Do We Love God?* Review last week's lesson to illustrate one way and then use rest of lesson on *prayer,* ending with a guided prayer meditation, and, perhaps, by making a chart or a booklet of the prayers we'd like to learn. Give out readings for next week's Thanksgiving liturgy.

Feast of Christ the King—Thanksgiving celebration should include either a liturgy or prayer service and a social moment. Offertory should include some sort of gifts from students—food for the needy, their prayer booklets, etc. Decorate room with things students have made and pictures for all.

Advent 1—Thanksgiving week often has no class, but if you do, use theme of "Waiting" to explain meaning of Advent. Begin Christmas songs and project.

Advent 2—*John Calls Us to a Change of Heart.* This is how we prepare for Jesus. Use Gospel for Advent 2 (Lk 3:1–6). Continue Advent or Christmas project and songs.

Advent 3—Read birth narratives and prepare for Christmas celebration next week.

Advent 4—*Christmas Celebration and Party.* Have a liturgy, prayer service or dramatic presentation of Gospel or any combination of these three. See suggestions.

Epiphany—Theme: *Jesus Came for All People East and West, North and South.* Use Epiphany Gospel (Mt. 2:1–12) to illustrate. Sing "He's Got the Whole World in His Hands" and "We Three Kings." Make posters with pictures of people of the world.

Baptism of the Lord—This Sunday is occasionally omitted, so check. Theme: *Baptism.* Use this day's Gospel (Lk 3:15–16, 2–22). Discuss children's baptism. Use ideas from Chapter 7.

2nd SIOT—Theme: *Confirmation and Baptism.* Use Reading I for 2nd SIOT on gifts of the Spirit (1 Cor 12:4–11). Begin singing confirmation songs: "Here I Am, Lord," "Peace Is Flowing like a River" (*Hi God II*) and "The Spirit Is Movin'" (Sadlier).

3rd SIOT—Theme: Continue *Confirmation and Baptism.* Use Reading II (1 Cor 12:12–14:27) on parts of body. Talk about how we become part of Church (body of Christ) in baptism and confirmation.

4th SIOT—Theme: *Eucharist.* Use feeding of the five thousand. Connect to confirmation and baptism—on nourishing the body of Christ. Sing "We Come To Your Table" (*Hi God II*) or "Take My Bread" or "I Am the Bread of Life."

5th SIOT—Theme: *Call of the Fishermen* (Lk 5:1–11). This would be a good week for a confirmation investiture service as the Gospel wraps up what you've been saying about confirmation and baptism. Songs could be "Here I Am, Lord" and others you know. Give each confirmation student a small gift such as a symbol of the Holy Spirit or a New Testament.

6th SIOT—Theme: *The Beatitudes* (Lk 6:17, 20–26). Contrast the call of Jesus to us in the beatitudes to the ten commandments.

7th SIOT—Theme: *The Beatitudes (continued)* (Lk 6:27–38).

8th SIOT—Theme: This is the third week that the Sunday Gospel readings develop the theme of the new covenant. Use explicit examples from the students' lives to illustrate the words of the Gospel.

9th SIOT—Theme: *On Faith.* Use Gospel for 9th SIOT (Lk 7:1–10), about the centurion. Show connection of centurion's words, "Lord, I am not worthy to receive you," to liturgy.

Lent 1—Theme: *Temptation.* Use Gospel (Lk 4:1–13) for Lent 1 about temptation of Jesus. Concentrate on how we are all tempted and how that is normal. Sing "Peace Is Flowing Like a River" (*Hi God II*) and "What Shall I Do?" (*Hi God II*) and "Sometimes It's Not Easy" (Sadlier 1).

Lent 2—Theme: *Forgiveness and Reconciliation.* Use story of prodigal son which is Lent 4 Gospel or story of the lost sheep (both Lk 15). Use Psalm 27 response, "The Lord is my light and my salvation," in prayer moment. Prepare for communal penance service next week.

Lent 3—Communal Penance Service. Use Gospel studied last week. Candles for all. Tie with purple ribbons.

Lent 4—Theme: *Last Supper.* See Chapters 2 and 6. Sing "We Come to Your Table."

Lent 5—Theme: Prepare for Palm Sunday or Holy Week liturgy or drama/role play way of the cross or the Last Supper.

Palm Sunday—Celebration and Social. Serve different kinds of bread. Sing "This Is the Day" (*Hi God II*) and "Allelu" (Ray Repp).

2nd SOE—Theme: *The Holy Spirit* (Jn 20:19–31). The risen Christ leaves the Holy Spirit with us to guide and strengthen us. Sing "Allelu" (Ray Repp).

3rd SOE—Theme: *Follow Me*. Use Gospel for week (Jn 21:1–19) with these words of Jesus to Peter and to us. Do guided prayer meditation, placing ourselves by the lake with Peter waiting to be addressed by the Lord.

4th SOE—Theme: *The Good Shepherd*. Use response for Psalm 100 for 4th SOE, "We are his people, the sheep of his flock." Sing Communion songs. Use this week to talk about the Church. Perhaps make poster for last celebration with pictures of all members of class around a picture of Jesus.

5th SOE—This week or next week would be an appropriate time for a final celebration; First Communion, confirmation or other. Use for theme commandment of Jesus to love one another from Gospel for this Sunday (Jn 13:31–35).

6th SOE—Theme: *Jesus Leaves Us the Holy Spirit To Instruct, Support and Guide Us* (Jn 14:23–29).

If you need additional lessons to finish your year's plan, the following are possible readings for the next few weeks.
Ascension—Lk 24:46–53
7th SOE—story of Stephen, the first martyr (Acts 7:55–60)
Pentecost—Acts 2:1–11

Plan 3—Using Cycle C to A

25th SIOT—Opening Liturgy. Theme: *Getting To Know You*. "Where two or three are gathered in my name, there am I in their midst" (Mt 18:20).

26th SIOT—Opening Liturgy as above or Theme: *God Calls Us Together To Serve*. Use Gospel for 26th SIOT, Lazarus and the rich man (Lk 16:19–31). Sing "Hurray for God" (Sadlier 1).

For prayer moment use response from 27th SIOT (Psalm 95),
"If today you hear his voice, harden not your hearts."

27th SIOT—Theme: *We Meet God in His Creation* (Gen 1:1–25).
Song: "He's Got the Whole World in His Hands" or "If I
Were a Butterfly" (*Hi God II*) or "Thank You, Lord, for All
Your Gifts" (*Hi God II*). Begin wall mural on creation using
pre-cut pieces that can be glued to a long piece of butcher
paper.

28th SIOT—Theme: *God Creates Man and Woman and Gives the
World to Their Care* (Gen 1:26–31). Songs as above and continue mural.

29th SIOT—Theme: *God Made Me and I Am Good* (Gen 2:4–7). Continue songs. Add pictures or stick figures of students to mural.

30th SIOT—*Creation Liturgy*. Display mural. Have children bring in
their favorite stuffed animals. Social afterward.

31st SIOT—Theme: *The Saints*. Meaning of Halloween (Holy Eve).
Use Gospel of 31st SIOT about Zacchaeus (Lk 19:1–10). We
are called to be saints—even a tax collector such as Zacchaeus. Sing "When the Saints Come Marching In." Have
a march. Make masks or signs for different saints.

32nd SIOT—Theme: *Thanking God for His Gifts*. Use Gospel for 27th
SIOT (Lk 17:11–19). "Thank You, God, for All Your Gifts"
(*Hi God II*). Discuss what God's gifts are (this is a summary
of previous lessons), and how we thank God for them.

33rd SIOT—Theme: *Prayer*. Continue from last week and discuss different kinds of prayer and how we pray. Distinguish between
memorized formal prayers and spontaneous prayer. Talk
about how we will do both this year. Make a prayer chart to
mark progress. Prepare for Thanksgiving celebration next
week. Send home readings to practice.

Feast of Christ the King—Thanksgiving liturgy—and possible food
collection and party.

Advent 1—Theme: *We Wait for Peace as Did the Prophets*. Use read-
ing from Old Testament for Advent 1 (Is 2:1–5). Start singing
Christmas songs and "Peace Is Flowing Like a River" (*Hi
God II*).

Advent 2—Theme: *How To Prepare*. Use Gospel for Advent 2 (Mt

3:1–12). Sing Christmas songs. Start preparing Christmas role play, liturgy, art project, etc.

Advent 3—Theme: *How Do We Know That Jesus Was God's Gift to Us?* Use Advent 3 Gospel (Mt 11:2–11). Sing Christmas songs and continue preparations for Christmas liturgy.

Advent 4—Christmas Liturgy. Pageant, party and/or play. Theme: *Jesus, Our Peace.*

Epiphany—Theme: *Jesus Comes for All Persons.* Use Gospel for Epiphany about visit of magi (Mt 2:1–12). Sing "His Banner Over Me Is Love" and "What Color Is God's Skin?" (*Hi God I*) and "We Three Kings." Do poster of people of many lands around a picture of Jesus.

Baptism of the Lord. This Sunday is omitted in several years. Check your lectionary. Theme: *The Call of Baptism and Confirmation.* Use Gospel for this feast (Mt 3:13–17). Sing "His Banner Over Me Is Love" (*Hi God I*).

2nd SIOT—Theme: *Here Am I, Lord.* Use psalm response (Ps 40) for this Sunday, "Here am I, Lord; I come to do your will." Continue discussion of baptism. Use Gospel for this Sunday (Jn 1:29–34).

3rd SIOT—Theme: *Confirmation.* Use the 3rd SIOT Gospel about the call of the fishermen (Mt 4:12–23). Sing "Here Am I, Lord" or other songs planned for confirmation, or "His Banner Over Me Is Love" (*Hi God I*) or "Kumbaya."

4th SIOT—Theme: *The Beatitudes.* Use Gospel for 4th SIOT (Mt 5:1–12). Develop theme in conjunction with responsibilities of the Christian (confirmation, baptism, etc.). Prepare a confirmation investiture for next week.

5th SIOT—Theme: *Confirmation Investiture Celebration.* This could be a liturgy, a prayer service or simply a short commissioning ceremony calling for a commitment on the part of the students to be confirmed. A social could follow. Using Gospel for 5th SIOT on the salt of the earth and the light of the world would be appropriate.

6th SIOT—Theme: *The New Covenant.* Contrast the ten commandments and the new covenant, using examples from this Sunday's Gospel (Mt 5:17–37). Continue singing songs for confirmation or Communion celebrations.

7th SIOT—Theme: *On Loving Your Enemy*. Use Gospel for 7th SIOT
(Mt 5:38–48). Practice various responses to violence or ill-
treatment in one's life in role-play.[1]

8th SIOT—Theme: *Faith (Trust in God)*. Use Gospel for 8th SIOT (Mt
6:24–34). For guided prayer meditation use Psalm 62.

9th SIOT—Theme: *Jesus, the Rock of Our Faith*. Use Gospel for 9th
SIOT (Mt 7:21–27). Sing "God Is Building a House" (*Hi
God II*).

Lent 1—Theme: *Temptation and Sin*. Use Sunday Gospel (Mt 4:1–11)
and Psalm 51 response for paraliturgy. Sing "Peace Is Flowing Like a River."

Lent 2—Theme: *Forgiveness and Reconciliation*. Sing "What Shall I
Do?" (*Hi God II*) and "Peace Is Flowing Like a River."

Lent 3—Communal penance service or prayer service for forgiveness
of sins.

Lent 4—Theme: *Jesus Heals*. Use Gospel for this Sunday (Jn 9:
1–41) on the healing of a blind man. Sing "Jesus, You
Have the Power To Heal" (*Hi God II*) or continue with
others.

Lent 5—Theme: *Jesus Dies for Us*. Review Passion story and prepare
for Palm Sunday (Easter) celebration, liturgy, role play of
Last Supper, or way of the cross dramatization.

Week before Palm Sunday or Easter—Celebration and Social. Serve
different kinds of bread and grape juice.

2nd SOE—Theme: *Jesus Sends the Holy Spirit*. Gospel for 2nd SOE
(Jn 20:19–31). Sing "Allelu" (Ray Repp), "This Is the
Day" (*Hi God II*) or "New Life" (*Hi God II*).

3rd SOE—Theme: *On the Road to Emmaus (On Recognizing Jesus)*.
Use Luke 24:13–35. Sing "God Is Building a House" (*Hi
God II*).

4th SOE—Theme: *Jesus Feeds Us*. Use Psalm 23 and the story of the
feeding of the five thousand, the Last Supper and a discussion
of Eucharist.

5th SOE—Theme: *Eucharist*. Continue last week's discussion and
make plans for final celebration and/or First Communion liturgy and breakfast or lunch.

6th SOE—Final Celebration. Sing favorite songs. Afterward give out
gifts or awards for all.

If you decide to continue your program after this week the following are the readings you might use for those weeks.
Ascension—Mt 28:16–20
7th SOE—Acts 1:12–14 on prayer
Pentecost—Ps 104 and Jn 7:37–39

Note

1. *Friendly Classroom for a Small Planet,* Order from Children's Creative Response to Conflict, FOR, Box 271, Nyack, N.Y. 10960. $6.95 plus $1 postage and handling.

Plan 4

For appropriate readings and music refer to similar lessons in Plans 1-3.

Week 1—Opening liturgy and social.
Theme: Back Together Again.
Week 2—God created the world and it is good.
Week 3—God created me in his image; I am good.
Week 4—God made us to live and love together; our families are our first community experience.
Week 5—We belong to many communities and one of these is the Church.
Week 6—We join the Church community through baptism.
Week 7—Baptism, Communion and confirmation (sacraments of initiation).
Week 8—Thanking God for his creation and the gift of each other (our communities).
Week 9—Thanksgiving liturgy and social. (Adjust your calendar so this falls just before Thanksgiving.)
Week 10—Waiting for Jesus.
Week 11—The call to change; the call to repentance.
Week 12—The birth of Christ; preparation for Christmas celebration.
Week 13—Christmas worship service and/or drama.
Week 14—Jesus came for all people (the magi—Epiphany).
Week 15—Jesus calls us to be his disciples.

Week 16—The old covenant—the ten commandments.

Week 17—The new covenant—the commandments to love God and neighbor.

Week 18—The beatitudes: Jesus especially loved the sick, the poor, the lonely and persecuted.

Week 19—The beatitudes (continued): the call to be peacemakers (on loving your enemy).

Week 20—Temptation and sin.

Week 21—Forgiveness and reconciliation.

Week 22—Jesus heals—healing liturgy.

Week 23—Jesus feeds us—the wedding at Cana.

Week 24—Jesus feeds us—the feeding of the five thousand.

Week 25   Jesus feeds us—the Last Supper and the Eucharist.

Week 26—Easter liturgy or way of the cross.

Week 27—Jesus sends the Holy Spirit: the Spirit of Jesus.

Week 28—On the road to Emmaus or "Follow me" from last chapter of John.

Week 29—Jesus the rock of our faith.

Week 30—On prayer.

Week 31—Final worship service (Communion or confirmation) and breakfast or lunch following with awards for all.

Appendix II

Liturgies and Prayer Services

To Catholics and to some Protestants a liturgy is a worship service composed of two parts: the Liturgy of the Word and the Liturgy of the Eucharist.

A prayer service, sometimes called a paraliturgy in this book, is a celebration of prayer and worship without the Liturgy of the Eucharist. It can have a variety of forms, but usually includes at least one Scripture reading, prayer and a response. It often also includes a litany, music, drama or role play, dance, and/or symbolic ritual.

Most paraliturgies (prayer services) can be celebrated without clergy participation. Therefore, if you want to have a liturgy, based on one of the following suggestions, but have no celebrant, just use the suggestions below and have a prayer service instead. Such a service is possible in any comfortable and reflective atmosphere.

In the samples below, I have listed readings for four persons so as to include as many students as possible. You may, of course, delete the second reading, the psalm and the prayer of the faithful if you wish and substitute a role play or Gospel dramatization for the Gospel if your celebrant is consulted and plans to be present.

These suggestions are brief and only intended to get you going. See bibliography for additional resources. Adapt!

1. Back Together Again: Opening Day Liturgy

Theme: "Where two or three are gathered in my name, there am I in their midst" (Mt 18:20)

Readings: *1st*—Psalm 23
Response—From Psalm 45, "The Lord is near to all who call upon him."
2nd—1 Cor 12:31–13:1–3, 8; 14:1
Gospel: Mt 18:19–20 or Mt 19:13–15
Prayer of the Faithful

Music:	"Back Together Again" (Sadlier 1)
	"This Is the Day" (*Hi God II*)
	"We Come to Your Table" (*Hi God II*)
	"His Banner Over Me Is Love" (*Hi God I*)
	"Kumbaya" ("Someone's Praying, Lord, Be With Us")
Special Notes:	This is appropriate for opening day or (without "Back Together Again" theme) as a liturgy celebrating community. Hang last year's pictures of everyone around celebrating area. Have coffee and doughnuts afterward. Invite family, friends, etc.

2. *Liturgy of Thanks for Creation* or *Celebrating Creation*

Theme:	"And God looked at everything he had made, and he found it very good" (Gen 1)
Readings:	*1st*—Gen 1 (selected creation verses)
	Response—From Psalm 8, "O Lord, our Lord, how glorious is your name over all the earth."
	2nd—St. Francis' *Canticle to All Creation*
	Gospel—Jn 1:1–4
	Prayer of the Faithful (Response: "We thank you, Lord.")
Music:	"He's Got the Whole World in His Hands"
	"If I Were a Butterfly" (*Hi God II*)
	"This Is the Day" (*Hi God II*)
Special Notes:	Have children decorate altar or room with their favorite stuffed animals. Make a creation mural to hang on altar. (See Lesson Plan 3)

3. *St. Francis Day Liturgy* or *Peace Liturgy* (Week of October 4)

Use similar format as above and perhaps add *Canticle to the Sun* and mural of St. Francis. St. Francis' Day could also be the occasion of a peace liturgy as he was a great pacifist. In this case sing "Peace Is

Flowing Like a River'' (*Hi God II*). Use, in this case, peace readings such as Isaiah 2:1–5 and John 20:19–29.

4. *Thanksgiving Liturgy*

Theme—	Giving thanks for all God's gifts or a time for sharing
Readings:	*1st*—Genesis 1 (selections)
	Response—A litany of thanks for God's gifts. Use response "Thank you, Lord" or use *Canticle to All Creation*
	2nd—2 Pet 1:1–4
	Gospel—Lk 6:36–38 or Lk 17:11–19
	Prayer of Faithful—Composed by children who take turns offering what they are thankful for.
Music:	"Thank You, Lord, for All Your Gifts" (*Hi God II*)
	"Hurray for God" (Sadlier I)
	"We Come to Your Table" (*Hi God II*)
	"Kumbaya"
	"His Banner Over Me Is Love" (*Hi God I*)
Special Notes:	Have attractive basket at altar and during offertory have children bring up food to be shared with the needy. Or have them bring something to share with and/or distribute to the whole group afterward.

5. *Advent Liturgy* (See Chapter 8)

Theme—	Jesus, Light of the World or We Wait for Jesus
Readings:	*1st*—Is 9:1 or Mk 1:1–3 or Mt 3:3 or 3:1–6
	Response—Ps. 130 (adapted). Use response "I wait for Jesus, my soul waits for him."
	2nd Reading—1 Thes 5:16–23 (adapted)
	Gospel—Jn 1:1–9 or Mt 11:2–11 (adapted)

Prayer of Faithful—Use "Lord, show us your light."

Music: "Prepare Ye the Way of the Lord" (*Godspell*)
"We Come to Your Table" (*Hi God II*)
"Come, Lord Jesus" (*Hi God II*)
"Silent Night"
"The People Who Walk In Darkness" (*Gentle Night*)

Special Notes: An advent liturgy would be especially effective in the evening when one could have a gradual lighting of the room; use candles for this.

6. *Christmas Liturgy* (See Chapter 8)

Theme—   Jesus, Our Peace. Happy Birthday, Jesus. The Birth of Jesus (Gospel Dramatization). Jesus, Light of the World or O Come, All Ye Faithful.

Readings: *1st*—Is 9:1
Response—Adapt Ps 97. Use "A light will shine on us this day."
2nd—Col 1:15
Gospel—Lk 2:15–20 and parts of Mt 2

Music: "O Come, All Ye Faithful"
"Silent Night"
"A Violet in the Snow," "Mary's Song," and "Come Lord Jesus" (*Hi God II*)
"The People Who Walk in Darkness" (*Gentle Night*)

Special Notes: See Chapter 8.

7. *Confirmation Investiture Liturgy*

Theme—   We Prepare To Answer the Call or Called To Be Christians in Word and Deed

Readings: *1st*— Jer 1 (the call of Jeremiah) or 1 Sam

Response: Ps 25, "Teach me your ways, O Lord" or adapt "Here am I, Lord" from 1 Sam

2nd—1 Cor 12:4–11 (adapted)

Gospel—Jn 15:9–15

Prayer of Faithful—Written for and by confirmands

Special Notes: Include an investiture ceremony in which candidates repeat baptismal promises (simplified) and receive a small gift appropriate to the occasion.

Music: "Hear, O Lord, the Sound of My Call"
"Here Am I, Lord"
"Let There Be Peace on Earth"
"Peace Is Flowing Like a River"
"This Is the Day"
"We Come to Your Table"
"His Banner Over Me Is Love" (*Hi God I*)

8. Jesus Helps Us

Theme— "The Lord is my shepherd, I shall not want," or "If God is for us, who can be against us."

Readings: *1st*—Ps 23

Response—Adapt Ps 146. Use response "Lord, come and help us." Or prepare your own litany, using this response.

2nd—Rom 8:26–27

Gospel—Jn 6:1–14 or Jn 10:11–16 (adapted)

Music: "Hear, O Lord, the Sound of My Call"
"Kumbaya"
"Joy, Joy, Joy" (*Hi God I*)

Special Notes: The way you structure and proceed with this liturgy will be determined by what context you use it in (i.e., how it fits in your year's plan).

9. The Way Which Surpasses All Others

Theme: Love—"Now I will show you the way which
                          surpasses all others" (1 Cor 12:31)

Readings: *1st*—Lev 19:1–2, 17–18
                          Response—Use Ps 90; response: "Fill us
                                  with your love, O Lord."
                          2nd—1 Cor 13:1–7
                          Gospel—Jn 14:21–23
                          Prayer of Faithful—Use response "We love
                          you, Lord."

Special Notes: This liturgy might be appropriate around Val-
                          entine's Day and the decorations and offer-
                          ings could reflect a heart's theme. It would
                          also be appropriate after a discussion and
                          contrast of the law and the new covenant (the
                          command to love). Use songs you have been
                          practicing plus "Kumbaya" (Someone's
                          Loving, Lord, Be with Us).

10. Communal Penance Service

Theme—   Reconciliation: This is not a liturgy, although
                          it could take place within one. A penance ser-
                          vice within the approved structure could look
                          like this.

                               I Introductory Rites
                                  Entrance Song—"Sometimes It's not
                                          Easy" (Sadlier) or
                                          "Hear, O Lord, the
                                          Sound of My Call"
                                          (Sadlier 4)
                                  Greetings and Opening Prayer
                              II Celebration of the Word of God
                                  Gospel: Lk 15:11–32 or Lk 15:1–6
                                  Homily
                                  Examination of Conscience—prepared
                                  by leader

III Rite of Reconciliation
All: I confess to almighty God,
and to you, my brothers and sisters,
that I have sinned through my own fault
in my thoughts and in my words,
in what I have done and in what I have
failed to do.
And I ask the blessed Virgin Mary, ever
virgin,
all the angels and saints,
and you, my brothers and sisters,
to pray for me to the Lord our God.
(Use this or some similar confession)
All: The Lord's Prayer
Song: "Someone's Praying, Lord, Be
With Us" ("Kumbaya")
Individual Confession
IV Prayer of Thanksgiving—Lighting of
candles
Song: "Someone's Loving, Lord, Be
With Us" or "Peace Is Flowing Like a
River"

Blessing and Dismissal

11. *Penitential Mass for Easter Season*

Theme— "Come back to me with all your heart" (Jl 2:12)

Readings: *1st*—Jl 2:12–13 (adapted)
Response—Use Ps. 130 (adapted). Response: "Lord, hear my voice"
2nd—Rom 8:5–7
Gospel—Acclamation "Change your lives, says the Lord." Lk 15:11–32 or Lk 15:1–6

Music: "Come Back to Me" (*Gentle Night*)
"Kumbaya," "How Great is Our God,"

"Sometimes It's Not Easy," "Hear, O Lord,
the Sound of My Call" (Sadlier)

12. *Looking Toward Easter*

Theme—   *The Promise*
Readings: *1st*—Is 52:13–15
                      Response—"Easter is the day that we have
                      been promised; let us rejoice and
                      be glad"
                      2nd—Lk 12:49–50
                      Gospel: Jn 11:25–27
Music: "This Is the Day," "How Great is Our
                      God," "Kumbaya," "Be Not Afraid,"
                      "We Come to Your Table," "Hurray for
                      God"

13. *Way of The Cross*—Not a liturgy

Theme—   In remembrance we walk with Jesus to the
                      cross.
Materials Needed: A fairly large area in which to set up fifteen
                      crosses. These could be of cardboard.
                      A crown of thorns and palms
                      A large wooden cross for Jesus to carry
                      Veronica's veil
                      A basin for Pilate's handwashing
                      Scarves for women's head or more elaborate
                      veils (costumes of Mary, etc.)
                      Soldiers' helmets, swords and capes or more
                      elaborate. For helmets use baseball hardhat
                      reversed and cover with foil.
                      White robe for Jesus
                      Hammer and nails
                      Tomb—a few sheets draped over chairs will
                      do
Directions: Rewrite these to suit your situation. Students,
                      parents, teachers walk from classroom with
                      palms. Pause in hallway to remember Last
                      Supper in a few words. At entrance to room

in which you are celebrating pause to remember agony in garden. *Enter room and walk to first station (first cross).*

Leader: And the soldiers brought Jesus before Pilate. (Soldiers pull Jesus toward Pilate, standing by a basin.) Pilate wanted to let Jesus go, but the high priests and the people shouted, "Crucify him." (Students cry "Crucify him" several times.) So Pilate washed his hands of the affair and condemned Jesus to death. (Pilate washes hands and points finger at Jesus.) The soldiers put a crown of thorns on his head and beat him. (pause)

Response: Jesus, we are sorry and we love you.
(all)

Walk to second station (second cross).

Leader: The soldiers made Jesus carry his cross to the place of crucifixion, and it was very heavy. (Soldiers have placed cross on Jesus who bends low under the weight.) (pause)

Response: Jesus, we are sorry and we love you.

Walk to third station (third cross).

Leader: Jesus was in so much pain and so tired that he fell. He could have called on God for help, but he didn't for he was willing to share our pain to show us how much he loves us. (pause)

Response: Jesus, we are sorry and we love you.

Walk to fourth station (fourth cross).

Leader: Mary has been looking for her son.

(Mary shields her eyes as if she is looking for someone.) Like all mothers she loves her son very much, and she is crying to see his pain. (pause)

Response: Jesus, we are sorry and we love you.

Walk to fifth station (fifth cross).

Leader: Jesus can't carry the cross anymore. He is too weak. So the soldiers make Simon of Cyrene help him. Think about how Simon was just grabbed from the crowd and has been remembered ever since for this. Jesus calls all of us to come out from the crowd and carry his cross with him. (pause)

Response: Jesus, we are sorry and we love you.

Walk to sixth station (sixth cross).

Leader: Veronica sees Jesus' pain and weeps for him. She takes her veil and wipes the sweat from his face. Do we weep for other people's pain as Veronica did for Jesus? (pause)

Response: Jesus, we are sorry and we love you.

Walk to seventh station (seventh cross).

Leader: Jesus falls again. Forgive us, Jesus, for the times we do not help those who stumble and fall and are in pain. (pause)

Response: Jesus, we are sorry and we love you.

Walk to eighth station (eighth cross).

Leader: The women of Jerusalem love Jesus for his gentle ways and because they can tell how much he loves their children, the poor, the sick, the hungry. Now they walk with him to keep him company in his pain. Do we also walk with those in pain? (pause)

Response: Jesus, we are sorry and we love you.

Walk to ninth station (ninth cross).

Leader: Jesus falls the third time. It's a long way to the cross. What is Jesus thinking about? Is he asking God to give him strength—to be with him? Do we always remember to ask God to give us strength and be with us? (pause)

Response: Jesus, we are sorry and we love you.

Walk to tenth station (tenth cross).

Leader: Jesus is stripped of his robe. The soldiers and the crowd are very cruel. They enjoy seeing someone-made fun of. Do we ever enjoy being cruel or embarrassing people as these people did to Jesus? If we do such a thing, are we not helping to crucify Jesus again? (pause)

Response: Jesus, we are sorry and we love you.

Walk to eleventh station (eleventh cross).

Leader: Jesus is nailed to the cross. Such pain we can endure only with the grace of God with us. Do we always pray for this grace in our pain? (pause)

Response: Jesus, we are sorry and we love you.

Walk to twelfth station (twelfth cross).

Leader: Jesus dies on the cross. After three bad hours, Jesus dies and his pain and humiliation are over. Now it is our turn to weep. What people do to each other! If we do not stand at the bottom of the cross and watch, we risk doing such things ourselves. (pause)

Response: Jesus, we are sorry and we love you.

Walk to thirteenth station (thirteenth cross).

Leader: Jesus is taken down from the cross and put in the arms of his mother. Now many people are weeping, for they begin to see what they have done. Before he died Jesus asked God to forgive them. Can they forgive themselves? Can we forgive ourselves for our past sins and move on to new life with Jesus? (pause)

Response: Jesus, we are sorry and we love you.

Walk to fourteenth station (fourteenth cross).

Leader: Jesus is laid in the tomb. Yes, Jesus is dead and everyone thinks this is the end. Now the world will never be saved from its evil. With Jesus their hope has died for a better world. (pause)

Response: Jesus, we are sorry and we love you.

Walk to fifteenth cross (in center of room; others have been around periphery).

Leader: But the burial, the tomb, was not the end. Three days after Jesus died, the tomb was found empty, and he appeared to Mary and Peter and John and many of his friends. Jesus lives and promises to be with us always until the end of the world.

Response: Jesus, we rejoice and we love you, for our hope is in you.
Sing: "This Is the Day" (*Hi God II*)

14. Easter Prayer Service

Theme—	*Hurray for God.*
Readings:	*1st*—Jn 13:1–15 (adapted)
	Response—"Easter is the day that we have been waiting for; let us rejoice and be glad."
	2nd—Phil 2:6–10 (paraphrased)
	Gospel—Mt 26:14–27
	Prayer of the Faithful: Take one thing that you hope for today and bring it to Jesus in prayer.
Music:	"Hurray for God" (Sadlier 1)
	"Allelu" (Ray Repp)
	"This Is the Day" (*Hi God II*)

15. First Holy Communion

Theme—	We Come to Your Table or This Is the Day or His Banner Over Me Is Love.
Readings:	*1st*—Ps 23
	Response—"This is the day that we have been waiting for; let us rejoice and be glad."
	2nd—Jn 6:48–51 (adapted)
	Gospel—Mk 14:22–26
Music:	"We Come to Your Table" (*Hi God II*)
	"This Is the Day" (*Hi God II*)
	"Take Our Bread" (Joe Wise)
	"His Banner Over Me Is Love" (*Hi God I*)
	"Hurray for God" (Sadlier)
Special Notes:	Have a Communion breakfast or lunch afterward and give out remembrances to all recalling something positive each has done in

the past year. Have programs with theme and names of communicants on the cover. Display pictures and other things made by students. Display photographs of students and class taken during year. Have each communicant make a banner with name and appropriate symbols to hang on altar and later in their rooms. Involve, if possible, all students in some way in this liturgy.

Appendix III

Suggestions for Workshops and/or Training Sessions for Teachers of Special Religious Education

Workshop 1

Introductory Workshop/Training Session/Meeting for New Teachers

Time: 2 hours plus time for refreshments and socializing

I. *Introductory remarks*—Welcome, purpose of meeting, hand out agenda. Note that the basis of this workshop is the material in Part I of this book as it defines what we're all about.

II. *Icebreaker*—Sharing later will be much improved if people get to know each other a little and a relaxed, non-threatening atmosphere is established. The following takes care of all of these if your group is no bigger than about 12–15. For larger groups use Workshop 4.

Sit in a circle and, starting with leader, give name and one thing you like to do. Next person repeats your name and thing you like to do and adds his/her own. Each successive person must repeat name and activity for all preceding persons adding his/her own last. As leader you go last also. This is a lot of fun and I guarantee you will know everyone's name when you are finished.

III. *On the Purpose of Special Religious Education*—Ask if anyone has had any experience in special education and inquire what if any ideas they have on the purpose of special religious education. Consider information in Chapter 1 on implementing discussion.

IV. *Presentation on three key concepts of Special Religious Education. Use Chapter 2.*

1. Affirmation and strategies therefore.
2. Community Building (How-to)
3. Getting To Know Jesus. This includes the key methodological concepts:
Use of Scripture and story
Prayer
Sacrament

Workshop 2

Second meeting/training session concentrates on your year and lesson plans. Several weeks or months before the opening of class would be a good time to have it. Time: 1¹/₂ to 2 hours.

I.   *Introductory remarks and agenda (as above).*

II. *Four Facts*—If you are going to be working together as a group it is important that you get to know each other better. This is an affirming and fun exercise which can help set a relaxed and amiable tone for the evening. There are two ways this can be done. Either simply go around in a circle and share four facts about yourself or in groups of two share four facts, and then take turns introducing each other to the larger group using these four facts.

III. *Explanation of how class will be structured* with a suggestion that volunteers begin thinking about how they would best fit into this structure.

IV. *Presentation of this year's plan* with some remarks on how it was developed and how we will proceed. Allow plenty of time for questions. (See Chapter 6.)

V.   *Preparing a lesson plan.* (Use Chapter 7.)

Workshop 3

Third Meeting—Time: 1¹/₂ to 2 hours

I.   *Introductory remarks*—Instead of an icebreaker ask people to share their feelings about what brought them here and a little of their expectations. This might include some remarks on how they hope to participate in the center.

II. *Presentation:* Introducing the Special Child. (Use Chapter 5.)

III. *Taking a list of your registered students,* talk about each student and his/her needs a little. Show pictures if you have any.

IV. *Distribute list of students* and the groupings which you have decided on and ask for volunteers to work with different groups.

Fourth meeting would be individual, explaining to each teacher how to work with his/her particular children and giving her the materials to do so.

Workshop 4

If you are doing a workshop for a diocese or a larger group of established teachers use workshop 1 ideas, but structure slightly differently.

Two hours or half a day with lunch. Leave plenty of time as people will want to keep talking.

I. *Introductory remarks* and passing out of agenda.

II. *Icebreaker*—If there are too many people for a circle ask participants to move to one of four corners of room depending on when their birthday is. One corner for January, February and March, another for April, May, and June, etc. Then ask them to face each other and share first their names and where they come from and then some non-threatening fact like one fun thing they did this summer. Then perhaps share something about why they are here today. (If groups have not turned out evenly, move a few people to achieve this.) As leader you answer each question first.

This can be continued by asking each group to count off by number and regroup all 1's, 2's, etc., and ask new questions in new groups. This is a little time-consuming, but well worth it. You are going to ask participants to break into small groups to address specific problems; therefore this is an important warmup for sharing.

III. *On the Purpose of Special Religious Education*
Ask participants to break into groups of three or four, preferably with people they don't previously know. Give each participant a pencil and paper on which are listed two questions.

1. What is the purpose of special religious education in the setting in which you are working?
2. How do you best implement this purpose?

Give participants a few minutes to think privately and write down their ideas. Then ask them to share their ideas with the others in the group (approximately 15 minutes).

Now ask one reporter from each group to report back to the larger group and record suggestions on chalkboard or newsprint.

IV. *Present your vision of the purpose* of special religious education and the three concepts of Chapter 2 relating the presentation to the remarks made. Be sure you present your Church's teaching and specific references for your opinions.

V. *Ask for evaluation of what has been said tonight.* This will probably occur spontaneously, but could be encouraged with remarks such as "Do you think we've been on the right track today?" or "What have you found most useful about our discussion this evening?"

If you are running out of time this could be written on a piece of paper and handed in anonymously.

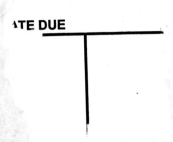